ELLE
VITALITY

ELLE

GUIDE TO HEALTH AND BEAUTY

VITALITY

BY KARENA CALLEN

LEOPARD

DEDICATION

To Mum,

Dad and Claire for their constant love, support

and faith.

And to Marty, for being my absolute tower of strength.

You have all been patient, understanding and loving

throughout.

ACKNOWLEDGEMENTS

All my thanks must go to everyone at ELLE, past and present, who has supported me from start to finish, and especially to Sally, Louise, Maggie, Annabel, Martin, Xavier, Clive, Charlotte, Geoff, Grant, and Jessica.

My love, thanks and appreciation must also go to Amanda Cochrane, for her wealth of knowledge and for sharing it so generously with me; to Jane Vernon-Lewis for being there when I most needed help; to Alex Templeton for her endless help, energy and enthusiasm; to Shelly Hunt for always being there; to Selina Marshall for her guidance and to Anna Maria Solowij for her wit and humour.

I would also like to thank all those who have contributed to this book in one way or another, especially the following:
Dreas Reyneke, Pemma Fox, Bridget Woods, Melanie Staples, Christina Hocking, Helena Champion, Lisbeth Russell, Lydia Wong, Jessica Roeb, Patrick Holford, Alexandra Hampton-Price, Kerry Sparkes, Cherie Arnold, Ellen Spann, Dr. Michel Odent, Laurie Starrett, Lesley Chilkes, Frances Hathaway, Miranda Joyce, Johnny Hernandez, Lucia Pieroni and Ruby Hammer. Last, but not least, a big thank you to all at Ebury, especially Fiona MacIntyre, and to Margot Richardson, Anne Johnson and Jerry Goldie.

Front Cover Credit
Photographer – Gilles Bensimon   Model – Elle MacPherson

This edition published 1996 by Leopard Books,
a division of Random House UK Ltd,
20 Vauxhall Bridge Road, London SW1V 2SA

First published 1991 by Ebury Press

Art Direction: Grant Scott and Geoff Waring
Design: Jerry Goldie
Picture Research: Alex Templeton

ISBN 0 7529 0043 9

CONTENTS

THE ELLE HEALTH & BEAUTY PHILOSOPHY

ELLE has always been associated with vitality. Call it energy, call it spirit, call it – as I know my French counterparts would – *joie de vivre*, vitality is not some kind of mysterious quality that is possessed only by a god-given few. But what is it? Are you born with it? Can you acquire it? These were just a few of the questions that I asked myself when I started writing this book. Vitality is a part of every person, and we are all capable of nurturing it and letting it transform our daily lives.

ELLE Vitality shows you how to bring out your *inner* vitality through a combination of diet, relaxation and massage while working on *outer* vitality with exercise, hair and skin care, and intensive body treatments.

My own philosophy is that health and beauty come only when the body, mind and spirit are in perfect harmony. This is not a new idea. In fact, it is the root of practically all the ancient healing philosophies from American native Indian to Aboriginal, from Chinese Taoism to Indian Ayurveda. If you look good, you will feel good and vice versa.

This is not a book about losing weight or dramatically altering your appearance. No amount of expensive skin care products or cosmetics can improve your outer appearance if you are dissatisfied within: they just won't work. But by learning meditation or yoga for example, or by indulging yourself once in a while with an aromatherapy massage, you can work on your inner 'self', on your emotional and spiritual side, as well as improving your physical body.

Spend just a few moments each day on yourself and use this book to explore your own vitality. It won't be long before you embrace the spirit of ELLE and liberate the vital energy within your own mind, body and soul.

The ultimate message of this book is that a perfect balance of all the aspects of well-being, when married together, can bring out your own vitality. It's a book about choice, individuality, modern health and beauty and, above all, a guide to help you achieve balance and vitality in your life.

CHAPTER ONE

EATING FOR ENERGY

T he ELLE health and beauty philosophy has always centred on vitality — vitality that stems from within. Through nutrition, it is possible to create a healthy mind and body. Our philosophy has never focused on weight loss diets, but rather on healthy eating plans. The priorities are to cleanse and rejuvenate your system, to gain vitality, and to rebalance your body. Of course, by following a well-balanced diet, it is obvious that you will shed a pound or two and, together with regular exercise and massage, who knows? — you may even noticeably reshape your body. Always bear in mind that nothing works independently. There is little point in putting all your energy into carefully planning what you are going to eat if you don't do any exercise or give yourself time to relax — that will only create an imbalance. Food is fuel — not only for the body but also for the mind. Without sufficient nutrients, both your psychological and physiological health will suffer.

So improve your well-being from within and start eating for energy.

A BALANCED DIET
HOW TO ACHIEVE VITALITY THROUGH NUTRITION

Balance is fundamental to our inner health and outer beauty. When mind, body and spirit are out of sync, we become unbalanced, resulting in a wide variety of different physical and psychological ailments.

Our bodies are constantly adapting – readjusting themselves to suit climate, environment, diet and even seasonal changes. Although we have powerful inbuilt rebalancers that control out temperature, hormone levels, blood pressure, digestive enzymes and energy levels, we cannot expect our bodies to work unaided.

Balance starts from within and, just as we need sleep, relaxation and exercise to maintain overall equilibrium, so we rely on food to provide the perfect balance of nutrients necessary for maximum health. Modern lifestyles often mean that our diet is not well balanced – that is, we do not have the correct proportion of vitamins, minerals, fats, carbohydrates, fibre, water and proteins to sustain peak performance. Hi-tech food processing and preparation leach food of vitamins and minerals and may provide us with no more than empty calories. Convenience foods and T.V. dinners may save time and effort but they are often stripped of essential nutrients that we actually need to preserve health and to boost our energy levels.

The result is a variety of complaints, including fatigue, poor digestion, lacklustre hair and skin, and inexplicable aches and pains. A balanced diet is a healthy diet and the only way to ensure that your body gets sufficient nutrients to maintain maximum health.

THE ELEMENTS OF A BALANCED DIET

The body is as complex as a sophisticated piece of machinery. It needs the correct balance of fuel in order to run efficiently and it needs variety. It is all too easy to fall into a routine when choosing your food and the fact that most of us have little time to spend planning menus and working out exactly what nutrients we need each day can lead to poor-quality nutrition. Although the body can survive on what you give it, you will not be able to achieve optimum health.

The main food groups on which we depend are proteins, carbohydrates, fats, vitamins and minerals, and each has a specific role to play in the maintenance of health.

PROTEINS

Proteins are the body's building blocks. All the body's main organs are created from protein, while hair, skin and bones also contain protein. Protein is required by these organs in order for them to function correctly.

When large amounts of protein are eaten, the body stores the excess in the muscles and organs. When people starve themselves or go on strict diets containing little or no protein, the body slows down the metabolic rate to compensate.

CARBOHYDRATES

The main source of energy, carbohydrates come in several forms. The simplest carbohydrates are glucose and fructose – single units of sugar. Then there are the complex carbohydrates, which are made up of a number of sugar units. Complex carbohydrates are found in vegetables, cereals and some fruits. They take longer to be broken down than simple carbohydrates and are therefore preferable, as they release their energy at a slower, more constant rate.

FATS

Like carbohydrates, fats or fatty acids are energy providers. They do, however, have twice as many calories as protein or carbohydrates for the same amount of weight. Although fats play an essential role, most people eat too much fat and there is increasing research to suggest that excessive fat intake is linked to coronary heart disease and to some types of cancer, in particular breast and colon cancers.

There are different types of fat – saturated, polyunsaturated and monounsaturated – some of which are more beneficial than others.

Saturated fats, derived from dairy products such as butter, milk, cream, lard, meat and some vegetable oils, are implicated in raised levels of harmful (LDL) cholesterol and are therefore the fats that most experts advise we eat in moderation.

Cholesterol is a fat found in eggs, dairy products and meat and although recent studies have pointed out the harmful effects of raised LDL cholesterol levels in the blood, cutting down on saturated fats is more advantageous to our general health than cutting out just the foods that contain cholesterol.

Unlike saturated fats, polyunsaturated fats,

found in safflower and rapeseed oils, seeds, nuts, vegetables and some fish, are thought to be beneficial. However, new research has found that polyunsaturate spreads and margarines may not be a better alternative to butter because of the chemical process, hydrogenation, used in their manufacture. Many experts therefore advise that we avoid margarines and other spreads containing hydrogenated fat.

Monounsaturated fats, as found in extra virgin olive oil, are thought to be the healthiest type of fats. Stable when heated, they are particularly suitable for cooking. Olive oil has also been found to be rich in antioxidants which guard against heart disease and cancer. It can therefore be used freely to make salad dressings and for stir frying.

VITAMINS AND MINERALS

Vitamins and minerals are essential in maintaining the body's metabolic function as they contain vital enzymes which control complex chemical reactions. Although there are a few vitamins and minerals that the body can manufacture itself, we rely on food to provide most of our essential supply.

While, undoubtedly, it is preferable to obtain vitamins and minerals from natural food sources, man-made supplements can help to protect us against certain forms of disease. When prescribed under supervision and used with care, vitamin and mineral supplements can be of valuable assistance to the body at certain times, such as during pregnancy, during and after illness, and in old age. There is one point, however, which needs to be stressed and that is that supplements are not intended to replace a well-balanced diet – they should only be used in addition to a sensible eating programme and not instead of one.

EATING FOR ENERGY

Do you always feel tired and lethargic? Do you feel that you need more than eight hours' sleep a night? Do you depend on coffee or tea to wake you up in the morning? Do you avoid exercise because you haven't got the energy? If you answered 'yes' to most of these questions, you need to look carefully at your diet.

Food provides your body with energy. Your body's mechanism to turn food into energy – the metabolism – is controlled by specific vitamins and minerals that play a vital role in its production.

Low energy is a sure sign of ill health. Many illnesses, such as cancer, infections such as thrush or cystitis, irritable bowel syndrome, headaches and migraine, eczema, asthma, PMS, high blood pressure and eating disorders, are early warning signals that demand you boost your energy levels with correct nutrition.

Energy is the product of a complex chain of chemical reactions in the body's cells. Controlled by enzymes, the glucose produced by carbohydrates is processed firstly into a chemical called pyruvic acid, and then into acetyl-coenzyme (AcoA). A series of chemical reactions isolates hydrogen molecules, which combine with oxygen to release energy. When the body's vitamin and mineral levels are depleted, energy production suffers and, in turn, we feel tired. The most important vitamins in the energy chain are the B complex. Without B1 and B3, glucose can't be converted into pyruvic acid, while AcoA can't be formed without B1, B2, B3 and B5. In addition, without B6, B12, folic acid and biotin, fats and proteins can't be transformed into energy when glucose levels are low.

The key for optimum energy is to eat sufficient amounts of complex carbohydrates - grains, beans, lentils and some vegetables – because they break down very gradually and release their sugar content slowly. Fruit, which contains fructose, is also slow-releasing.

Avoid sugar and most sweeteners, which are fast-releasing, as are biscuits, cakes and white bread, whose processing and overcooking have already turned their complex carbohydrates into simple sugars. As they require little digestion, they release their sugar content rapidly into the bloodstream. The blood sugar level rises too quickly, often giving a noticeable boost to energy, then the body races to lower the blood sugar level to avoid flooding it and the level plummets, causing a drop in energy one to three hours after eating.

Too much refined sugar often results in glucose intolerance – an inability to maintain even blood sugar levels. Symptoms include fatigue, irritability, dizziness and insomnia. Stimulants have much the same effect as sugar because they stimulate the release of glucose into the blood. The first step to improving energy is to cut out, or cut down on, stimulants, including coffee, tea, chocolate, sugar and refined foods, cigarettes, fizzy drinks and alcohol, and to increase your intake of complex carbohydrates.

THE PROPERTIES AND SOURCES OF ESSENTIAL VITAMINS AND MINERALS

VITAMIN A
Vitamin A helps to protect the body's tissues against bacterial and viral invasion. A poor supply of vitamin A can result in skin blemishes and doctors have found it beneficial in treating minor cases of acne, eczema and psoriasis in addition to scalp disorders. It is also essential for maintaining the cells of the retina in the eye, and deficiencies of the vitamin can result in deterioration of the eyesight. It is also thought to have anti-stress properties.

SOURCES
Carrots, broccoli, parsley, spring greens, spinach, cabbage, eggs, fish liver oils, liver. Most fruit and vegetables contain varying amounts of vitamin A.

VITAMIN B COMPLEX
Made up of several individual vitamins, the B complex also works together to help maintain brain function and the body's nervous system. Also essential for a clear complexion and a lustrous head of hair.

SOURCES
Although it is made in the body, external sources include fruits and vegetables, whole grains, pulses, liver.

VITAMIN B1 (thiamin)
Thiamin helps to convert carbohydrates into energy and is essential to the nervous system and to a healthy heart. Thiamin also alleviates fatigue and stress and too little can lead to depression and irritability.

SOURCES
Liver, pork, green vegetables, potatoes, beans, whole grains.

VITAMIN B2 (riboflavin)
Like thiamin, riboflavin helps to convert carbohydrates into energy. It is essential for healthy skin, scalp, eyes and mucous membranes. It helps to strengthen the adrenal glands and protects them from the effects of stress.

SOURCES
Cereals, wheatbran, pulses, green leafy vegetables.

VITAMIN B3 (niacin)
Assists in the production of energy from carbohydrates, fats and protein. Also essential for brain and nervous system functions and for maintaining healthy skin, tongue and digestive organs.

SOURCES
Liver, kidneys, fish, yeast, milk, cheese, eggs, whole grains, vegetables, fruit.

VITAMIN B5 (pantothenic acid)
Used in the breakdown of food for energy. This vitamin is important in preserving the body's natural tolerance to stress. It is also used in the production of antibodies, which protect the body from infection. Produced by the body via intestinal bacteria, which manufacture it in substantial amounts.

SOURCES
Whole grains, liver, kidneys, eggs, fresh vegetables, brewer's yeast.

VITAMIN B6 (pyridoxine)
This vitamin is thought to alleviate depression and has been used to treat premenstrual tension. It is used in the body to metabolise protein and amino acids, which are essential for healthy functioning of the brain and nervous system. It is thought that the Pill, smoking and alcohol all deplete the body's store of B6, and supplements may be a wise precaution.

SOURCES
Liver, whole grains, fish, bananas, pulses, potatoes, sunflower seeds, nuts such as hazelnuts and peanuts.

VITAMIN B12 (cyanocobalamin) and FOLIC ACID
Essential for the production of haemoglobin, in conjunction with folic acid, which is another member of the B complex. In addition, B12 and folic acid are both involved in energy production and help to boost the immune system. Only small amounts of these B vitamins are required but vegans and vegetarians are susceptible to deficiency. The Pill can often deplete natural supplies of B12 and folic acid, so supplements may be necessary.

SOURCES
Liver is a good source of both vitamins. B12 is present in kidneys, meat, milk, sardines, oysters, salmon and cheese, while folic acid can be found in whole grains, leafy green vegetables and fruit. One of the most interesting sources of B12 is spirulina, a blue-green algae that nutritional experts recommend as a dietary supplement because of its exceptional concentration of nutrients.

VITAMIN C
A natural anti-oxidant, vitamin C plays a role in the absorption of iron and in the production of hormones in the adrenal glands. It is thought to protect the body against disease by boosting the immune system and helps to prevent skin damage by strengthening the skin's collagen fibres. Many experts believe that vitamin C can act as a powerful anti-pollutant and that it can help the body to dispose of harmful elements such as lead.

SOURCES
Potatoes, green peppers, green vegetables, citrus fruits, rose hips, blackcurrants, acerola cherries, tomatoes.

VITAMIN D
Made in the skin when the body is exposed to sunlight, vitamin D is essential for healthy bones, nervous system, the eyes and the heart. Vitamin D is essential in the absorption of calcium and is thought to protect from osteoporosis.

SOURCES
Tuna, salmon, fish liver oils, mackerel, egg yolks.

INSTANT ENERGY BOOSTERS
The quickest way to boost your energy is also, in the long run, the least effective. Sugary snacks, cakes and chocolate may get your level up for a short time, but the rush does not last. Instead, look to raw vegetable crudités, nuts and seeds, fresh fruit and delicious energy-boosting cocktails. Boost your energy with a cocktail of carrot, apple, lemon and orange. Blend four carrots with three apples, one lemon and one orange, or combine carrot and celery, or beetroot and carrot, for a delicious and therapeutic drink. In addition to raw juices, protein drinks can also help to build up your flagging energy levels and provide essential vitamins and minerals. Blend together 450 ml (¾ pint) of freshly made apple juice with the juice of one pear, 75 g (3 oz) of plain tofu, 2 tbsp ground cashewnuts and ½ tsp of cinnamon. Or combine 600 ml (1 pint) soya milk with 75 g (3 oz) tofu, (4 oz) 100 g blackberries, strawberries or raspberries and 1 tsp honey.

FUEL FOR ENERGY
Fresh vegetables and fruit, pulses, lean fish, poultry and meat, wholegrain cereals, plus small amounts of dairy produce and nuts, in that order, should form the mainstay of a healthy diet that's geared towards optimum energy and vitality, as well as to helping the body settle at its ideal weight. Forget calorie counting – it is not only impractical and inaccurate, but encourages eating obsessions. Moreover, nutritionists have discovered that, while a daily intake of 1,000 calories may shift pounds for one person, it can have little or no effect for another. It's all due to individual variations in metabolic rate – the efficiency with which the body is able to turn calories into energy. People who have a high metabolic rate rarely complain of weight problems.

It's also thought, though not 100 per cent proven, that when food is in short supply, metabolic rates fall as the body attempts to main-

VITAMIN E
An anti-oxidant, it helps to protect the body's cells from damage by peroxides, marauding elements formed in the breakdown of polyunsaturated fats. It is also required by the main glands, such as the pituitary and the adrenals, for hormone production.

SOURCES
Green leafy vegetables, corn, whole grains, wheatgerm, egg yolks.

VITAMIN K
The function of vitamin K is to assist in blood clotting. It is manufactured in the body by intestinal bacteria.

SOURCES
Green leafy vegetables, sprouts, peas, liver, live yoghurt, milk, blackstrap molasses.

MINERALS
CALCIUM
Calcium is required in large amounts by the body to maintain the health of teeth and bones, in addition to assisting in blood clotting, heart function and general body repair.

SOURCES
Dairy products, yoghurt, kelp, watercress, sprouted grains and seeds.

COPPER
Essential for the formation of ribonucleic acid (RNA) and elastin, copper is an important part of the body's natural healing mechanism.

SOURCES
Meat, fish, seafood, whole grains, lentils, seeds, pulses, fruits.

CHROMIUM
Helps to control blood sugar level. The active form is known as GTF – glucose tolerance factor. Deficiency may lead to arterial disease and thrombosis.

SOURCES
Black pepper, liver, molasses, cheese, wheat bran, oysters, whole grains, cereals.

IODINE
A constituent of thyroxine, the hormone produced by the thyroid gland, which controls the metabolism.

SOURCES
Seaweed, especially kelp, iodised salt, fish liver oils, seafood, beans.

IRON
Vital for the production of blood haemoglobin and muscle myoglobin, and for the cytochromes of the respiratory system. Iron also aids in the metabolic production of protein and helps prevent fatigue.

SOURCES
Green leafy vegetables, molasses, whole grains, seafood, liver, meat.

MAGNESIUM
A natural tranquilliser, magnesium is also needed for the absorption of the minerals calcium and phosphorus.

SOURCES
Seafood, apples, dried fruits, green vegetables, corn, soya, brown rice, bran, figs, grapefruit.

MANGANESE
Used in the metabolism of fat and carbohydrates, manganese is also needed in the production of hormones and by the nervous system.

SOURCES
Leafy green vegetables, tea, beans, whole grains, egg yolks.

POTASSIUM
Potassium helps to maintain the body's acid-alkali balance and in regulating the body's levels of water in the cells and tissues. It also plays a role in the transmission of nerve impulses.

SOURCES
Potatoes, dried fruits, wheat bran, whole grains, molasses, bananas.

SELENIUM
Another anti-oxidant, selenium works in harmony with vitamins C and E to protect the body from pollutants. Recent research has highlighted the role of selenium in the prevention of certain forms of cancer.

SOURCES
Whole grains, cereals, seafood, meats, fish, tomatoes, broccoli, onions, liver.

SODIUM
Working in conjunction with potassium, sodium is abundant in our diet. It plays a role in the blood and nervous system and is essential to the muscles and the lymphatic system. Too much sodium has been linked to hypertension or high blood pressure and it can also encourage water retention.

SOURCES
Used as a preservative, sodium is present in most manufactured foods. It is also present in poultry, bread, seafood.

SULPHUR
An essential constituent of healthy hair, skin and nails, sulphur is involved in the manufacture of red blood cells. Sulphur deficiency is rare, as there are many sources.

SOURCES
Fish, beans, beef, onions, sprouts, leafy green vegetables.

ZINC
This trace mineral plays a role in a variety of enzyme-controlled functions and is essential for physical, mental and sexual development. Zinc deficiency is thought to be linked to anorexia nervosa and supplements of the mineral are used to treat the illness. It is also thought that zinc, in conjunction with vitamin C, can protect the body against the cold virus.

SOURCES
Seafood, whole grains, root vegetables, pulses.

tain equilibrium. So, when you start to eat normally again, weight goes back on faster. This type of slimming also results in feelings of depression, irritability and lethargy. It is far more desirable to be aware of the quality and quantity of what you eat than to become obsessed by calorie counting.

THE ELLE VITALITY EATING PLAN
Like most healthy diets, the ELLE vitality plan is based on nutrient-rich foods. Fresh vegetables, fruits, fish, whole grains, plus small amounts of nuts and seeds form the mainstay of this 10-day plan.

But this diet goes one better by creating an awareness of the best combination of foods for efficient digestion. Complex carbohydrates, such as breads, cereals and grains, are known to be a key source of energy. These foods must be broken down by enzymes before being absorbed as simple sugars into the bloodstream and taken to cells all over the body. Here they are processed further by other enzymes to produce energy. The operation comprises a chain of complex chemical reactions and is subject to set backs along the way.

Poor digestion is a major stumbling block. Tension, generated by anxiety, irritability, anger and frustration, interferes with the free flow of digestive enzymes, so eating when overwrought or exhausted often results in indigestion and provides little in the way of energy.

The programme features fish, a primary source of amino acids – which are the main constituents of the enzymes involved in energy release in the digestive system. Fish is, generally speaking, much easier to digest than other protein-rich foods, and recent concern about antibiotics and growth hormones used in cattle meat and dairy and poultry farming makes it a wise choice.

The emphasis is on dishes containing oats, pulses and fish, as they have a positive rebalancing

effect. Fish is also a good source of potassium and zinc (needed to make digestive enzymes), iodine (which controls the rate at which food is metabolised), plus other minerals and trace elements essential to energy-releasing enzymes. Being low in fat, white fish is an ideal food for anyone wishing to shed excess pounds, as long as it is grilled, baked or poached rather than fried.

The recipes concentrate on low fat and high carbohydrate foods to boost energy levels. Complex carbohydrates mentioned earlier, such as breads, cereals and grains, are infinitely preferable to simple carbohydrates, found in sugar, sweets, chocolates and biscuits. Sugar provides only 'empty' calories, as there is no accompanying fibre, minerals, vitamins – that is, no nutrutive value whatsoever. Any sensible diet should avoid refined sugar whenever possible.

In addition to grains and pulses, the diet focuses on fruit and vegetables. Choose fresh fruit and vegetables, preferably organic, and keep food preparation to a minimum. Fruit and vegetables have a cleansing action, encouraging toxic wastes to be eliminated.

Don't be alarmed if your skin breaks out in the odd spot initially – it just shows that the eating plan is working. Drinking plenty of mineral or spring water also helps flush the wastes out of the system. By the end of the ten days, your skin should look brighter and clearer than before.

CLEANSING EATING PLAN

Dietician Helena Champion has devised this 10-day eating plan to replenish the body's energy supplies. The diet is in two parts. The diet for the first three days will cleanse the digestive system and restore it to its full potential, aiding proper absorption of nutrients. The following seven-day diet then aims to re-educate your palate towards a healthier way of eating. The recipes are designed to encourage a more imaginative way of preparing food and to ensure a high mineral, vitamin and fibre content and low fat and sugar levels. As well as revitalising the digestive system, the plan may even help you to lose a pound or two.

When you've got to the end of the 10-day plan, instead of resuming your old eating habits, use the latter seven-day period as a stepping stone towards a more nutritious diet. It will take more effort on

your part than using convenience foods but the results may convince you that it is worthwhile.

Foods should be in their natural state, rather than tinned or pre-cooked. Use fresh fruit and vegetables whenever possible and, to attain the highest levels of vitamins, minerals and fibre, eat vegetables raw or only lightly cooked.

When preparing meals, use sugar sparingly and only in conjunction with fruits or whole grains to prevent too rapid absorption by the body. Fats should also be kept to a minimum. Use polyunsaturated oils and spreads in preference to saturated fats like butter. For sauces and dressings, choose low-fat curd cheese and yoghurt whenever possible.

SPROUTED LEGUMES

Sprouted seeds and pulses are recommended by Champion as a rich source of raw protein, vitamins and minerals. They are ideal for adding variety and are excellent digestive cleansers. To sprout pulses and seeds, soak the beans or seeds in plenty of water for 18 hours. Pour off the excess water, cover with a cloth and place in a warm, dark place. Rinse the beans twice a day and ensure that they do not stand in water as this can allow moulds to grow.

Once the seeds have sprouted, leave them on a window sill in the light for a few hours before eating. Beans such as mung, chickpeas and whole lentils take three to five days to sprout. Seeds such as sunflower, sesame and pumpkin sprout more quickly – between one and two days.

Many health food shops sell ready-sprouted seeds and pulses, such as alfalfa and bean shoots.

RAW POWER

Eating raw vegetables or salad before a meal aids the digestion and the absorption of nutrients. You could prepare a selection of crudités and a low-fat cheese or yoghurt dip, or experiment with vegetable juices. These are usually more palatable when mixed, the best bases being carrot, spinach, celery, cucumber and beetroot. If you don't have a juice extractor, ready-made vegetable juices are available in health food shops.

To gain the full benefits of the eating plan, try to cut out tea, coffee, alcohol and smoking. You should drink at least eight glasses of fluid a day, including fresh fruit and vegetable juices and spring water.

HEALTHY EATING GUIDELINES

● **Choose fresh fruit and vegetables when possible.**
● **Snack on fruit if hungry, but wait at least an hour after a meal.**
● **Replace whole milk with skimmed or semi-skimmed. Better still, try goat's milk.**
● **Drink no more than three cups of tea or coffee daily. Try to replace them with herbal tisanes, fresh juices and mineral water.**
● **Drink only freshly squeezed juice.**
● **Keep a diary of the foods you eat each day to make you more aware of what you're eating.**
● **Decide what is a reasonably sized portion and try not to keep on eating until you are full.**
● **Try to eat a large proportion of raw or lightly cooked vegetables and retain the cooking juices for use in the recipes.**
● **Supplement your diet with fresh fruit and vegetable juice.**
● **If you are addicted to a hot drink first thing in the morning or during the day, opt for herbal teas or hot water with freshly squeezed lemon or lime juice. Add honey to sweeten.**
● **Use minimal amounts of fat for cooking and ensure that servings of starch-based foods, such as breads, rice, potatoes and pasta, are generous.**
● **Don't despair if you are overcome by the desire to eat chocolate, or whatever your favourite indulgence may be. Have what you want – but in moderation.**

THE 10-DAY CLEANSING PLAN

DAY 1
BREAKFAST
A selection of fresh fruit, fruit juice or mineral water

LUNCH
As breakfast

DINNER
As breakfast

DAY 2
BREAKFAST
Large fresh fruit salad
Natural yoghurt

LUNCH
Mixed salad with sliced avocado and sprouted seeds
Vegetable juice
Fresh fruit

DINNER
Gazpacho (see recipes)
Mixed salad with sprouted seeds
Fresh fruit

DAY 3
BREAKFAST
Large fresh fruit salad
Natural yoghurt

LUNCH
Mixed salad with sprouted seeds
Vegetable juice
Fresh fruit

DINNER
Pot Barley Soup (see recipes)
Mixed salad with avocado and sprouted wheat
Herbal tisane or spring water

DAY 4
BREAKFAST
Toast with grilled tomatoes
Fresh fruit salad
Herbal tisane or spring water

LUNCH
Salad, Butter Bean Soup (see recipes), wholemeal bread
Low-fat yoghurt with honey

DINNER
Swedish-Style Trout and Crisp New Potatoes (see recipes)
Baked apple with cinnamon

DAY 5
BREAKFAST
Fruit salad
Muesli with milk or yoghurt
Spring water

LUNCH
Chicken and Bean Salad (see recipes), pitta bread
Low-fat yoghurt with honey

DINNER
Grilled Lamb Fillet with Rosemary, Crisp New Potatoes (see recipes)
Wholemeal apricot crumble or fresh fruit

DAY 6
BREAKFAST
Fruit salad
Omelette with fresh herbs, wholemeal bread
Fresh fruit juice or herbal tisane

LUNCH
Mixed salad, Stilton and Herb Pâté (see recipes), jacket potato
Fruit

DINNER
Fish Kebab with Brown and Wild Rice (see recipes)
Fresh fruit salad

DAY 7
BREAKFAST
Fruit salad
Muesli with milk or yoghurt

LUNCH
Bulgar wheat pilaff
Fresh fruit
Spring water

DINNER
Baked Tarragon Trout with Crisp New Potatoes (see recipes)
Baked Apple with Raspberries (see recipes)

DAY 8
BREAKFAST
Fruit salad
Toast with grilled tomatoes
Herbal tisane

LUNCH
Sprouted salad, jacket potato
Low-fat yoghurt with honey

DINNER
Halibut Steaks au Poivre (see recipes), new potatoes
Fruit with low-fat yoghurt

DAY 9
BREAKFAST
Fruit salad
Muesli with milk or yoghurt

LUNCH
Torn Vegetable Salad (see recipes), wholemeal bread
Fruit

DINNER
Stir-fried Prawns with Crisp New Potatoes (see recipes), Banana baked with cinnamon and honey

DAY 10
BREAKFAST
Fruit salad
Poached egg and toast

LUNCH
Tuna Coleslaw (see recipes), jacket potato
Fruit

DINNER
Chicken Juliette (see recipes), wholewheat pasta
Yoghurt and strawberry whip (blend yoghurt, 1 banana and a few strawberries, and sprinkle with nuts)

Use this menu plan as a guideline for your own favourite foods, or follow these recipes.

FISH KEBABS WITH BROWN AND WILD RICE
(Serves 4)

110 g (4 oz) wild rice
225 g (8 oz) salmon steaks
4 scallops
8 langoustines, shelled, or 225 g (8 oz) monkfish, filleted
4 red mullet, filleted
2 large red peppers, washed and trimmed
2 courgettes, washed and trimmed
2 yellow courgettes, washed and trimmed
50 ml (2 fl oz) white wine
juice of 2 lemons
1 tsp ground white pepper
25 ml (1 fl oz) sunflower oil
1 tsp coriander seeds, crushed
550 ml (18 fl oz) fish stock, from trimmings
110 g (4 oz) brown rice
50 g (2 oz) parsley, chopped
salt and pepper
radicchio and curly endive, to garnish

Soak wild rice in cold water – overnight if possible. Cut each type of fish and seafood into eight equal rounds. Cut peppers and courgettes into bite-sized pieces.

For each kebab, thread a bamboo skewer with pieces of fish and vegetable as follows: scallop, pepper, red mullet, courgette, salmon, yellow courgette, langoustine (or monkfish), pepper. Repeat and end with a piece of scallop.

Mix together wine, lemon juice, white pepper, oil and coriander, and marinate kebabs for up to 2 hours. Pour fish stock into a saucepan and bring to the boil. Add brown and wild rice, bring back to a simmer and cover.

Meanwhile, place the kebabs on a baking sheet and grill for 10–12 min, turning occasionally. When rice is cooked, put on a baking sheet, add parsley, season and mix. Place on warmed plates with one kebab on each and garnish with radicchio and curly endive.

STILTON AND HERB PATE
(Serves 4)

25 g (1 oz) butter

50 g (2 oz) Stilton cheese

150 g (5 oz) low-fat curd cheese

pinch of mixed herbs

1 tbsp chopped parsley

salt and pepper

4 leaves red lettuce

12 leaves chicory

1 bunch watercress

1 tbsp chopped parsley, to garnish

Melt the butter in a pan, add the Stilton, curd cheese, herbs and half the parsley. Blend and season. Arrange on individual plates and garnish with salad leaves and parsley.

GAZPACHO
(Serves 4)

110 g (4 oz) onions, peeled and roughly chopped

110 g (4 oz) cucumber, trimmed and roughly chopped

110 g (4 oz) peppers, trimmed and roughly chopped

600 ml (1 pint) tomato juice

300 ml (½ pint) orange juice

dash of lemon juice

60 g (2½ oz) fresh breadcrumbs

dash of red wine vinegar

1 clove garlic, peeled and crushed

salt and pepper

50 g (2 oz) mixed peppers, finely diced, to garnish

Place onions, cucumber and peppers in a liquidiser and blend until smooth. Add tomato juice, orange juice, lemon juice, breadcrumbs, vinegar, garlic, salt and pepper. Blend, chill and serve cold, sprinkled with peppers.

BUTTER BEAN SOUP
(Serves 4)

1 vegetable stock cube

900 ml (1½ pint) water

225 g (8 oz) butter beans, soaked overnight

1 small onion, peeled and chopped

1 clove garlic, peeled and crushed

pepper

pinch of caraway seeds, to garnish

Dissolve stock cube in water and add butter beans, onion and garlic. Simmer for about 1 hour, until beans are tender. Blend until smooth and adjust seasoning. Garnish with caraway seeds.

POT BARLEY SOUP
(Serves 2)

75 g (3 oz) pot (wholegrain) barley

2 tbsp corn oil

1 large onion, peeled

2 cloves garlic, peeled

3 medium carrots, scrubbed

2 medium potatoes, scrubbed

3 stalks celery, washed

1 bay leaf

1 tsp mixed herbs

2 tbsp shoyu (naturally fermented soy sauce)

1 vegetable stock cube

450 g (1 lb) tomatoes, ripe (or tinned)

freshly ground black pepper

1 tbsp fresh parsley, chopped, to garnish

Wash the barley and soak in 600 ml (1 pint) cold water for at least 4 hours or overnight. Drain liquid into a measuring jug and add enough water to reach a level of 900 ml (1½ pints). Heat the oil in a heavy-bottomed saucepan and sauté the onion and garlic gently for about 5 min until soft. Stir in drained barley and cook for 3 min. Add the reserved water, bring to the boil, cover and simmer for 20 min. Meanwhile, slice carrots into thin rings and the potatoes and celery into thin slices. Add them to the cooking barley along with the bay leaf, mixed herbs, shoyu and stock cube. Cook for 10 min. Skin the tomatoes, if fresh, by immersing in boiling water for 5 min and then covering with cold water. Chop or liquidise tomatoes to a smooth consistency. Pour this into the soup and cook until potatoes and carrots feel soft. Add pepper, garnish with parsley and serve.

SWEDISH-STYLE TROUT
(Serves 4)

4 × 225 g (8 oz) trout, cleaned and gutted

50 g (2 oz) oat flakes

150 ml (5 fl oz) natural yoghurt

2 tbsp honey

2 tbsp lemon juice

2 tbsp creamed horseradish relish

1 eating apple, cut into small pieces

salt and pepper

110 g (4 oz) red pepper, finely diced

2 tbsp chopped parsley, to garnish

Remove heads and fins, and roll trout in oat flakes. Place on lightly greased baking sheet.
Blend together yoghurt, honey, lemon juice and horseradish. Add apple. Season to taste and pour on to four plates.
Grill trout for 10–15 min. Place one on each of the beds of yoghurt sauce. Heat trout on plates under the grill for 1 min, being careful not to overheat as sauce will separate. Garnish with red pepper and parsley.

STIR-FRIED PRAWNS
(Serves 2)

2 tbsp corn or peanut oil

2 spring onions or 5 cm (2 in) leek, cleaned and finely sliced

1 medium carrot, peeled and diced

1 small green pepper, diced

1 small red pepper, diced

1 clove garlic, peeled and finely sliced

1 tbsp fresh ginger, peeled and grated

50 g (2 oz) button mushrooms, wiped and sliced

110 g (4 oz) mangetout, topped, tailed and halved

25 g (1 oz) mung bean sprouts

25 g (1 oz) cashew nuts

200 g (7 oz) frozen prawns, defrosted

1 tbsp shoyu (naturally fermented soy sauce)

Heat oil in a wok or frying pan. Quickly fry the onions or leek, carrot, green and red peppers, garlic and ginger for 2 min, turning the mixture constantly. Add the mushrooms, mangetout and bean sprouts. Fry for 1 min. Add the cashew nuts and prawns and fry for 1 min, still turning constantly. Mix in the shoyu and serve immediately.

TUNA COLESLAW
(Serves 4)

110 g (4 oz) white cabbage, finely shredded

25 g (1 oz) pineapple, fresh or canned in natural juice and chopped

1 tomato, skinned, de-seeded and chopped

2 anchovy fillets, finely sliced

110 g (4 oz) dolphin-friendly tuna in brine, drained and flaked

2 tsp olive oil

2 tsp white wine vinegar

salt and pepper

25 g (1 oz) chopped chives, to garnish

Mix together cabbage, pineapple, tomato, anchovy fillets and flaked tuna. Put oil and vinegar in a jar and season with salt and pepper. Shake until well mixed, pour over salad and toss well. Serve garnished with chives.

THE 10-DAY CLEANSING PLAN

HALIBUT STEAKS AU POIVRE
(Serves 4)

4 × 150 g (5 oz) halibut steaks

salt

150 ml (5 fl oz) natural yoghurt

1 tbsp lemon juice

1 tsp honey

freshly ground black pepper

50 g (2 oz) mixed carrots, leeks and celery, peeled, trimmed and diced

300 ml (½ pint) fish stock

50 g (2 oz) onion, finely chopped

50 ml (2 fl oz) dry white wine

25 g (1 oz) wholemeal flour

25 ml (1 fl oz) water

½ tsp Dijon mustard

1 bunch watercress to garnish

Place halibut steaks in an ovenproof dish and season lightly with salt. Mix together yoghurt, lemon juice and honey and pour over fish. Sprinkle with black pepper.
In a saucepan, add vegetables to fish stock and simmer. Strain through a muslin cloth and reserve stock. Discard vegetables. In a pan, briskly cook the onion with the wine until liquid has evaporated, being careful not to burn the onion. Add stock and bring to boil.
Mix flour with water into a fine paste. Whisk flour paste into boiling stock, add mustard and simmer for 20 min, to reduce the stock.
Grill halibut for 15 min, turning once, until light brown. Serve fish on a bed of sauce with a garland of watercress leaves.

BAKED TARRAGON TROUT
(Serves 2)

2 sprigs of fresh tarragon

4 thin slices lemon

2 × 350–450 g (12 oz– 1 lb) rainbow trout, cleaned and gutted

white pepper and small pinch of salt

2 large sheets of newspaper-weight kitchen paper (available from catering trade suppliers)

juice of 1 lemon

Place 1 sprig of tarragon and 2 lemon slices in the cavity of each fish. Dust lightly with white pepper and salt. Place one trout at corner of each sheet of paper. Wrap them up, folding the corners in halfway to form an envelope. Wet the parcels thoroughly under the cold tap. Place them on a rack in the centre of the oven, preheated to Gas Mark 5 (190°C/375°F). Cook for 20–25 min or until paper has dried out.
Using scissors, cut open the envelopes and peel away the paper – this should lift the skin off the trout. If it does not lift away, scrape it gently with a knife. Place fish on a preheated plate and pour over the lemon juice.
NB If you prepare and cook an extra trout this can be cooled and used the next day in the fish and vegetable salad.

CHICKEN JULIETTE
(Serves 4)

600 ml (1 pint) chicken stock

15 g (½ oz) caraway seeds

4 × 150 g (5 oz) chicken breasts, skinned

110 g (4 oz) carrots, peeled and roughly chopped

110 g (4 oz) onion, peeled and roughly chopped

salt and pepper

110 g (4 oz) fresh spinach, shredded

1 clove garlic, peeled and crushed

4 small cauliflower florets

4 small broccoli florets

parsley, chopped, to garnish

Pour half the chicken stock into a frying pan. Add half the caraway seeds and poach chicken breasts in this liquid for 30–35 min. Keep warm.
In another saucepan simmer the chopped carrots and half the onion in 150 ml (¼ pint) stock until soft.
Transfer this mixture to a liquidiser and blend until smooth. Season to taste with salt and pepper.
In the last 150 ml (¼ pint) stock, simmer the shredded spinach with the garlic and remaining onion for 2 min.
Transfer this mixture to a liquidiser and blend until smooth. Season to taste with salt and pepper.
Blanch cauliflower and broccoli florets by plunging them into boiling water for 15 seconds and then placing in cold water immediately afterwards. Warm plates. Pour a semi-circle of each of the sauces on to the centre of each plate. Place a poached chicken breast in the middle of this and sprinkle with the chopped parsley and remaining caraway seeds.
Garnish each plate with florets of broccoli and cauliflower.

BULGAR WHEAT PILAFF
(Serves 2)

75 g (3 oz) frozen sweetcorn

1 vegetable stock cube

¼ tsp turmeric

110 g (4 oz) bulgar wheat (also called cracked wheat)

2 tbsp corn oil

1 medium onion, peeled and chopped

1 medium carrot, peeled and diced

1 stick celery, sliced

1 clove garlic, peeled and crushed

1 small green pepper, seeded and diced

1 small red pepper, seeded and diced

50 g (2 oz) whole almonds, skinned

¼ tsp ground coriander

¼ tsp ground cumin

¼ tsp paprika

crushed seeds from 5 cardamom pods

50 g (2 oz) button mushrooms, wiped and sliced

1 tsp mixed dried herbs

1 tbsp chopped fresh parsley

1 tbsp lemon juice

Cook sweetcorn in boiling water for 3 min and drain. Pour 300 ml (½ pint) boiling water into a heatproof bowl and dissolve the stock cube. Stir in turmeric, then bulgar wheat. Leave to stand for 30 min, then drain. Heat oil in a frying pan and fry onion, carrot, celery, garlic, green and red peppers and almonds briskly for 2–3 min, turning frequently. Add coriander, cumin, paprika and cardamom seeds. Fry for 1 min. Add mushrooms and sweetcorn, fry for 1 min, then add the soaked bulgar wheat, dried herbs and parsley. Fry for 1 min, turning the mixture to prevent burning. Add lemon juice and serve.

CALVES' LIVER WITH RED WINE
(Serves 4)

2 tbsp sunflower oil

350 g (12 oz) organic calves' liver, in four thin slices

25 g (1 oz) wholemeal flour

50 g (2 oz) onion, peeled and chopped

75 ml (3 fl oz) red wine

4 tbsp tomato purée

75 ml (3 fl oz) water

pepper

broccoli florets, blanched, to garnish

Heat oil. Dust liver with flour and lightly fry in oil until sealed. Place liver in an ovenproof dish and soften onion in the remaining juices.
Pour in wine and reduce by half. Add tomato purée and water, stirring well. Season and pour over liver.
Cover and bake for 1 hour at Gas Mark 4 (180°C/350°F). Arrange on plate and garnish with broccoli.

TORN VEGETABLE SALAD
(Serves 4)

75 g (3 oz) spring onion

75 g (3 oz) white cabbage

75 g (3 oz) red cabbage

75 g (3 oz) spinach

75 g (3 oz) Cos lettuce

75 g (3 oz) parsley sprigs

1 bunch watercress, washed and trimmed, to garnish

Dressing

25 g (1 oz) Stilton cheese

50 ml (2 fl oz) skimmed milk

25 ml (1 fl oz) lemon juice

salt and pepper

Tear all the vegetables except the watercress into a large, chilled bowl and toss well. Blend together all the dressing ingredients. Spoon over salad and toss. Garnish with torn watercress.

CRISP NEW POTATOES
(Serves 4)

1 tbsp sunflower oil

450 g (1 lb) small new potatoes, scrubbed and dried

pinch of rosemary

fresh ground black pepper

Preheat oven to Gas Mark 5 (190°C/375°F). Heat oil in a roasting dish. Put potatoes in dish and coat with oil. Sprinkle with rosemary and pepper. Roast for about 1 hour, until golden brown.

CHICKEN AND BEAN SALAD
(Serves 4)

110 g (4 oz) cooked chicken breast

110 g (4 oz) kidney beans, soaked and cooked

110 g (4 oz) chickpeas, soaked and cooked

50 g (2 oz) leeks, finely sliced

50 g (2 oz) red pepper, diced

50 g (2 oz) mushrooms, finely sliced

1 tbsp honey

1–2 tbsp lemon juice

pinch of cayenne pepper

pinch of paprika

salt and pepper

parsley, chopped to garnish

Shred chicken breast. Mix together with kidney beans, chickpeas and vegetables. Add honey, lemon juice, cayenne pepper and paprika. Season and mix well, then garnish with parsley.

BAKED APPLE WITH RASPBERRIES
(Serves 4)

4 well-shaped cooking apples, washed and cored

50 g (2 oz) brown sugar

50 g (2 oz) sultanas

pinch of cinnamon

4 cloves

225 g (8 oz) raspberries, washed

Remove the core of each apple. Place in an ovenproof dish. Sprinkle with brown sugar, sultanas, cinnamon, cloves and raspberries. Add about 1.25 cm (½ inch) water.
Bake in a preheated moderate oven, Gas Mark 3 (160°C/325°F), for about 1 hour, basting the apples occasionally until their skins have turned golden brown.

LIQUID ASSETS
DRINK YOUR WAY TO HEALTH

Coffee and, to a lesser extent, tea both contain caffeine, which is a highly addictive stimulant. In large quantities, it can have unpleasant side-effects, including headaches, jumpiness, anxiety and irritability. Furthermore, a possible link between excessive caffeine intake and breast cancer is currently being investigated. De-caffeinated coffee is not necessarily the answer, as the caffeine may have been extracted by chemical solvents.

HERBAL TISANES

Herbal tisanes are the ideal replacement as they contain no harmful additives or stimulants. Like many herbal remedies, they can also offer relief from many minor ailments. The wide variety of aromatic flavours and their individual healing properties provide an almost never-ending choice to suit every palate and need. Herbal tisanes are made from dried herbs, fruits and flowers and, like most things, they should be taken in moderation. If you need a hot drink while you are working, try to alternate between spring water and tisanes throughout the day.

You can buy tisanes ready-made, either in teabag form or loose from herbalist suppliers and health food stores. If you have a garden, you can grow your own herbs and make up fresh tisanes from the leaves, flowers and roots where appropriate.

Although you can use herbs, plants and flowers for a wide variety of purposes, the main way to reap their rewards is to brew up infusions and decoctions. An infusion, also known as a tea or tisane, is made by placing 25 g (1 oz) of the dried herb, flower or root in a teapot, to which 600–900 ml (1–1½ pints) of boiling water is then added. Leave to brew for about eight to 10 minutes and then drink. You can add honey or fruit juice to taste – fresh lemon or lime juice often enhances the flavour of tisanes. Some infusions, such as peppermint, rosehip, chamomile and fennel, are delicious when they are chilled. Add ice and lemon juice for a refreshing and therapeutic drink in hot weather or as an alternative to carbonated drinks. Serve with a slice of lemon, lime or orange.

Decoction is used to prepare drinks from the roots and bark of plants. Add 25 g (1 oz) of the root or bark to 900 ml (1½ pints) of water, place in a saucepan, bring to the boil and then simmer for between 15 and 20 min. Dilute with hot water or add honey or fruit juice to taste as with an infusion.

FRESH JUICES

Ensure that you are getting a rich supply of essential vitamins, minerals and enzymes by drinking freshly made fruit and raw vegetable juices.

The internationally renowned researcher and

THE PROPERTIES OF TISANES

ANISEED
Aniseed is known for its aromatic fragrance and taste. Soothing and decongesting, it can aid dry coughs and helps to calm digestive upsets. Crush the seeds to make a soothing tisane.

CHAMOMILE
Chamomile is widely recognised as having soothing and calming properties. It contains blue azulene, which is anti-inflammatory, calms digestive upsets, relaxes the nervous system and promotes restful sleep.

DANDELION
A well-known diuretic, dandelion leaves contain potassium, essential for healthy function of the heart. Dandelion tea can be used to treat sluggish kidneys, urinary infections or pre-menstrual fluid retention.

ECHINACEA
The root of this plant can be used to ward off viral, fungal and bacterial infections. It has a double action against infections and apparently works both by destroying harmful organisms and by encouraging the body's immune system. Useful for cleansing the body and for fighting infections such as tonsillitis and bronchitis. Make a decoction by simmering 15 g (½ oz) of the root in 600 ml (1 pint) of water for 15–20 min.

FENNEL
Fennel seeds can be infused to make an excellent tisane that aids digestion. By stimulating a sluggish digestive system and by soothing discomfort such as flatulence and cramping pains, it is the perfect antidote to indigestion. Reputed to reduce craving for nicotine. Avoid during early pregnancy.

FEVERFEW
Used for centuries to cure a plethora of aches and pains, the leaves of the feverfew can be brewed up into a tea, which helps to alleviate headaches, especially migraines. It acts as an anti-inflammatory and has been found to be beneficial in the treatment of arthritis and minor joint injuries.

GINGER
An excellent cure for nausea, particularly motion and morning sickness, ginger root also boosts the blood circulation, helping to warm the body, especially in cold weather. Slice up fresh ginger and infuse for a few minutes in boiling water. You can use powdered ginger although it is obviously not so potent.

LEMON BALM
The leaves of the lemon balm make a curative tea, which can be used to treat indigestion, colic and flatulence. It is also a soothing drink for those who suffer from stress or nervous disorders.

doctor, Norman W. Walker, discovered the healing properties of juices over 70 years ago when he was researching the relationship between diet, illness and longevity. Walker believed that a healthy diet should comprise at least 70 per cent raw fruit and vegetable juices and that we should eat only a small proportion of cooked foods. He stressed the importance of juices because they are easy for the body to assimilate quickly and efficiently, taking on average only 10–15 min for the body to digest.

Invest in a juicer or a versatile food processor, which will allow you to experiment with different fruits and vegetables, as they possess various healing properties. Scientists have discovered that carrots and dark green leafy vegetables contain carotinoids, which protect the body against cancer, fight infection and promote a healthy complexion. Celery is thought to detoxify and cleanse the system, while beetroot builds up the red corpuscles in the blood. It is best to combine vegetable juices or to add lemon or orange juice. If the juice is too strong, dilute with a little spring water. Boost your immune system with a cocktail of carrot, apple, lemon and orange. Blend four carrots with three apples, one lemon and one orange, or combine carrot and celery, or beetroot and carrot, for a delicious and therapeutic drink.

In addition to raw juices, protein drinks can also help to build up your natural defences. Blend together 450 ml (¾ pint) of freshly made apple juice with the juice of one pear, 75 g (3 oz) of plain tofu, 2 tbsp ground cashewnuts and ½ tsp of cinnamon. Or combine 600 ml (1 pint) of soya milk with 75 g (3 oz) tofu and 110 g (4 oz) blackberries, strawberries or raspberries with 1 tsp honey.

Boost your energy levels and create your own fresh juice cocktails rich in essential minerals and vitamins.

LIQUORICE
Liquorice root has an anti-inflammatory action and is particularly useful for treating digestive problems, such as ulcers. It acts on the adrenal glands in a similar way to the body's own natural hormones. Its expectorant qualities make it a useful treatment for chest infections. Avoid using liquorice if you have high blood pressure, as it has a similar action to steroids.

LIME BLOSSOM
Also known as linden blossom, it is rich in essential oils and helps soothe sore throats and coughs. Lime blossom also reduces fever and soothes fraught nerves.

NETTLE
Rich in minerals and vitamins, especially iron and vitamin C, nettles are excellent cleansers and act by stimulating blood circulation and improving kidney function. Nettles are also used in the treatment of skin disorders, such as psoriasis and eczema. Relieves exhaustion and stress.

PASSIONFLOWER
An instant relaxant, passionflower – or passiflora – aids sleep and relieves nervous tension and stress. Take in the evening to promote sleep or to help you relax after a stressful day. Avoid passionflower if you are pregnant, as it may stimulate the muscles of the uterus.

PEPPERMINT
Famous for its therapeutic effect on the digestive system, peppermint is soothing and calming. It can also be used to eliminate fevers as it encourages perspiration, so helping to lower body temperature. Use the leaves to make a delicious tisane.

RASPBERRY LEAF
Useful before and during menstruation to soothe discomfort and in the late months of pregnancy as it is thought to help tone uterine muscles but should be avoided in early pregnancy. Also helps to soothe sore mouths and throats.

VALERIAN
Known for its natural tranquillising properties, valerian can be used to relieve insomnia and to treat nervous disorders and stress. It is also thought to help lower high blood pressure but should be used in moderation, as high doses can be stimulating, rather than relaxing.

ELDERFLOWER
Elderflowers contain bioflavinoids, which help to strengthen blood vessels. Helps to ease sore throats and loosen catarrh. It also acts as a diuretic and has a cleansing effect on the digestive system. It helps to boost the circulation and encourage perspiration and is therefore useful for easing colds and 'flu.

THERAPEUTIC PROPERTIES OF FRESH FRUIT JUICES

APPLE
Rich in vitamins A and C and in magnesium and potassium, recent scientific studies have suggested that apples possess a number of healing properties. Researchers at the University of Paul Sabatier, in Toulouse, reported that a regular intake of apples appeared to lower LDL (harmful) cholesterol levels, while boosting HDL (beneficial) cholesterol. Dr. Sable-Amplis believes that it is the pectin present in apples that helps to break down cholesterol. Although apples are rich in natural fruit sugar, they do not cause a sharp rise in blood sugar levels.

BANANA
An excellent source of vitamin A, bananas are also rich in vitamin C and potassium. According to Professor A.K. Sanyal of Banaras Hindu University, Varanasi, India, and Dr. Ralph Best of the University of Aston, Birmingham, bananas have a soothing and healing effect on stomach ulcers and may, in fact, help to prevent duodenal ulcers.

CRANBERRY
Rich in vitamins A and C, cranberries have been shown to protect against urinary and kidney infections. The berries appear to possess anti-bacterial properties, which help to keep infections at bay.

GRAPE
Grapes are particularly rich in vitamin A but also contain vitamin C and high levels of niacin and potassium. They have been reported to have special healing powers for centuries, as they contain such a wide range of nutrients. Many researchers claim that they have potent anti-viral properties as they contain tannins, which help to cover inflamed tissues with a protective surface.

GRAPEFRUIT
Ultra-rich in vitamin C and to a lesser extent in vitamin A, grapefruit pectin contains potent polysaccharides, which help to lower harmful blood cholesterol levels. A high level of vitamin C in grapefruit is also thought to help protect the body against certain forms of cancer by boosting the body's immune system.

LEMON
Again rich in vitamins A and C, lemons possess similar therapeutic properties to grapefruit. A natural anti-oxidant, lemon juice is an effective preservative and, when added to other fresh fruit juices, helps to preserve their potency. Lemon juice and hot water is an excellent 'cleanser'.

ORANGE
Not as rich in vitamin C as the grapefruit, oranges do, however, have a higher level of niacin and potassium. The pectin contained in oranges helps to fight against arterial disease and high cholesterol levels and it is also thought that the fruit contains similar anti-cancer properties to grapefruit.

PAPAYA
Rich in vitamins A and C and a wide range of minerals, this tropical fruit is now widely available. Papaya contains papain, which is similar to the digestive enzyme found in the human stomach known as pepsin. It appears to improve digestion and to have a healing effect on the digestive organs. Papaya juice also has a healing effect when applied externally to wounds.

PRUNE
Very rich in vitamin A, prunes also contain useful amounts of thiamin, niacin, potassium and magnesium. Known for its laxative properties, prune juice is best used in moderation – half a glass each day is sufficient.

JUICE COMBINING
Fruit juices can be used in combination to enhance both taste and therapeutic value. Although it is a matter of taste as to which combinations you prefer, try some of the following – grapefruit, orange and lemon; papaya and orange; cranberry and apple. Add a little honey, yoghurt, oat bran and wheatgerm to create energising cocktails.

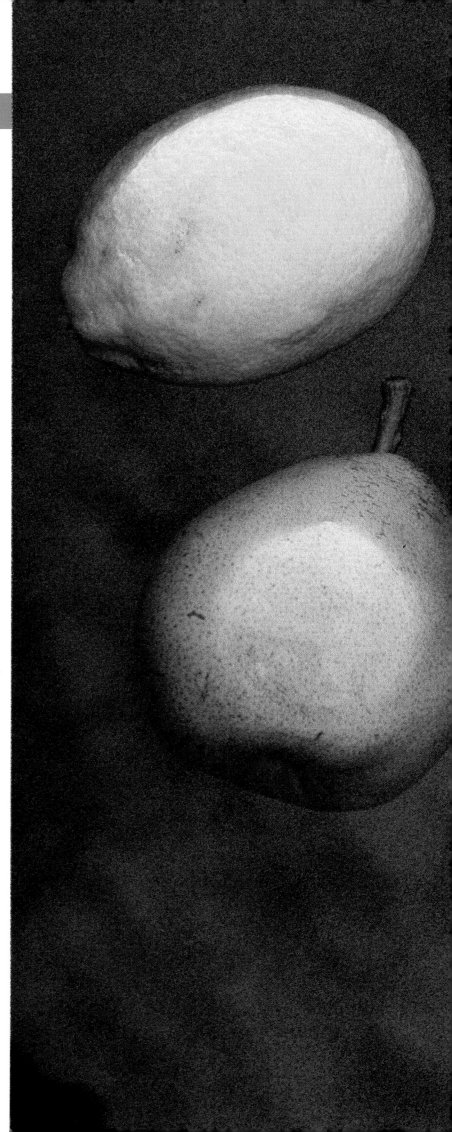

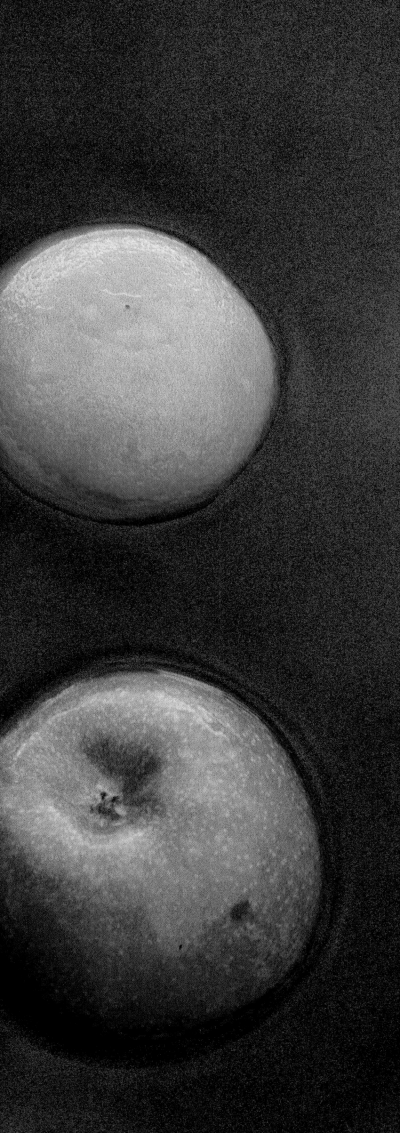

THERAPEUTIC PROPERTIES OF FRESH VEGETABLE JUICES

ALFALFA
Containing a very high level of vitamin A, alfalfa is also a good source of vitamin C, thiamin, riboflavin, calcium and potassium. Rich in chlorophyll, alfalfa has been found to build up the body's natural resistance against disease. Best combined with carrot juice, alfalfa juice is rich in restorative nutrients.

BEETROOT
A good source of vitamins A and C, niacin and potassium, beetroot juice helps to build up the red corpuscles in the blood and is particularly beneficial when taken during menstruation. Blend it with carrot or cucumber juice and dilute with spring water to taste.

CARROT
Carrots offer a plentiful supply of vitamins A, B, C, D and E, niacin and potassium. Recent research shows that carrots are rich in betacarotene, which has been shown to protect the body's cells against certain forms of cancer – particularly lung and cervical cancer. It also thought that carrots strengthen the immune system, fight against infection and protect against digestive disorders. Mix it with apple and lemon juice for a delicious and nutritious drink. Take carrot juice in moderation. According to juice expert, Dr. Norman Walker, the cleansing effect of carrot juice, coupled with the high level of betacarotene it contains, can lead to discoloration of the skin.

CELERY
High in vitamins A and C, celery is a rich source of organic sodium, which helps to maintain the body's calcium level. Celery is also high in magnesium and iron, both of which are essential for blood production. Combine it with carrot juice for health-enhancing benefits.

CUCUMBER
A good source of vitamins A and C, cucumber is known for its diuretic and cleansing properties. High in minerals, research has shown it to have a positive effect on rheumatic ailments and on high blood pressure.

GARLIC
A good source of vitamins and minerals, garlic has cleansing and protective effects, which have been well documented for centuries. Scientific evidence has proved garlic to have powerful anti-bacterial properties and that it also acts as an immune system booster. It's best not to use your juicer to make garlic juice – wrap a piece of muslin around a garlic press to get a teaspoonful of juice. Add the juice to a glass of carrot and lemon juice to make it more palatable.

LETTUCE
Rich in the minerals magnesium and iron, and in chlorophyll. The iron content in lettuce juice aids liver and spleen function, while the magnesium benefits the nervous system.

SPINACH
Very rich in vitamins A, C and E, spinach is also a good source of niacin and calcium. It has mild laxative properties and helps to cleanse and revitalise the colon.

TOMATO
Tomato juice contains vitamins A and C, potassium, sodium, calcium and magnesium. It also contains a high level of lycopene, a betacarotene, which researchers believe protects against cancer.

JUICE COMBINING
Vegetable juices are more difficult to combine than fruit juices, mainly because they tend to be bitter and not quite so appetising. However, by blending small amounts of juice, you can find combinations that suit your taste. Also add spring water, herbs, a little sea salt or lemon juice. The following work well: carrot, lettuce and alfalfa; carrot and spinach; carrot, beetroot and cucumber; celery, lettuce and spinach. You can also combine vegetable and fruit juices. Try carrot and apple, or tomato and lemon.

PROTECTION FROM POLLUTION

No matter how much effort we may put into cleaning up the planet and protecting our immediate environment, pollution is a problem that we cannot avoid. Environmental scientists have warned us against the growing strength of ultra-violet light and we are being encouraged to cover up and take extra precautions when exposed to strong sunlight. But it is not just the depletion of the ozone layer that we need to worry about. Everyday pollutants such as car fumes, cigarette smoke, and electromagnetic radiation from satellites, televisions and computers can all take their toll on our general state of health.

Researchers have estimated that in one year the average person consumes 12 pounds of food additives, has a gallon of pesticides sprayed on the fruit and vegetables that he or she eats, receives nitrates, hormone and antibiotic residues in both water and food, and breathes in two grams of solid pollution.

Experts have now suggested that pollution can weaken our immune system, so lowering our resistance to illness. Many studies have proved a link between pollution exposure and an increased risk of disease such as cancer, M.E., M.S. and a variety of minor ailments and allergies. So what can we do to safeguard our health?

Although we have powerful in-built adaptors, which help our bodies to acclimatise to external hazards, our systems can become overloaded, increasing the need to boost our natural defences. Early warning signs can include drowsiness, mood swings, blemished skin, headaches and nausea, allergies and frequent infections. The only way to fight pollution within the body is to increase our supply of anti-pollutants through our diet. Nature has provided us with powerful protectors such as vitamins A, B-complex, C and E, and the minerals zinc, selenium and calcium. These nutrients increase the body's own detoxifying capacity, so ensuring that it works efficiently. Most pollutants are 'anti-nutrients' – they interfere with the absorption of essential nutrients. The main hazards to avoid include toxic metals such as lead, aluminium, cadmium and mercury; free radicals, dangerous oxygen molecules produced by ultraviolet light, heat, combustion and frying foods; nitrates and pesticides; and drugs and food additives. (See Pollution Checklist.)

Ensure that you are getting sufficient quantities of protective vitamins in your diet (see vitamin and mineral section, page 12) to bolster your natural resistance and to detoxify your system. If you feel that your diet lacks any of the correct nutrients, make an effort to eat at least some of the anti-pollutant-rich foods as often as possible. If your lifestyle is such that you have little time to incorporate variety, then seek advice about the supplements that you may require.

It is also advisable to ensure that your diet contains sufficient fibre or roughage as this too has been shown to have a protective effect. It would appear from the latest research that fibre can absorb many harmful toxins by 'vacuuming' them out from the digestive system, so aiding the excretion process. This ensures that they are not allowed to linger in the body where they could accumulate. Increase your intake of dietary fibre, such as oatbran, porridge (ideal for those with wheat sensitivity), cereal, fresh fruit and vegetables.

NATURAL IMMUNE SYSTEM BOOSTERS

The immune system is the body's first line of defence in protecting the body against disease and harmful external elements. The immune system does not work unaided and factors such as diet, relaxation, exercise and stress can all influence our natural immunity positively or negatively. Recent research suggests that, just as we can protect ourselves from pollution, so we can also bolster our system against disease by building up the immune system.

The most important vitamins and minerals for immune system function are vitamins A, B complex, C and E, essential fatty acids, and the minerals iron, selenium and zinc. Amino acids, the body's protein-building blocks, are also important in the complex chain of chemical reactions that protect the body by stimulating the brain's natural pharmacy of health-promoting substances, such as tyrosine, tryptophan and glutamine.

PROTECTING YOUR IMMUNE SYSTEM

Avoid eating foods high in cholesterol and in saturated fats. Ensure that your diet is high in dietary fibre such as fresh fruit and vegetables, whole grains, beans and pulses. Cut down your intake of simple carbohydrates, such as sugar, cakes and sweets. Increase your consumption of complex carbohydrates, such as brown rice, whole wheat, corn and potatoes. Reduce your intake of caffeine, found in coffee, tea, cocoa and cola-type drinks. Do not smoke, and limit your intake of pharmaceutical drugs and alcohol.

POLLUTION CHECKLIST
● Avoid foods packaged in aluminium foil and aluminium cooking pots and pans; and don't wrap or cook food in foil.
● Choose organic fruit and vegetables whenever possible.
● Always wash fruit and vegetables with plenty of cold water.
● Don't smoke and encourage people around you to stop too – passive smoking can be just as harmful.
● If you cycle or jog in traffic, wear a protective face mask which helps to filter out toxins.
● Use filtered water and drink bottled water in preference to tap water.
● Keep your consumption of pre-packaged and convenience foods to a minimum.
● Avoid foods that contain additives.
● Keep sun exposure to a minimum and limit, if not avoid, the use of sunbeds.
● Check that you are using lead-free paint when decorating your home.

CHAPTER TWO

EXERCISE

Exercise is an integral part of ELLE's health and beauty philosophy. It is essential for mind, body and spirit in order to maintain perfect equilibrium. In a world that is increasingly based on materialism, and a lifestyle that has become increasingly fast and furious, few of us have the leisure time we really need to unwind and to revitalise. A compilation of ELLE's best body-shaping and conditioning exercise programmes, designed by experts to give maximum results in minimum time, allows you to choose the activity best suited to your lifestyle. Safe, fast and effective, these programmes can be tailored to your own needs and to the amount of time that you have to spend on body maintenance. From gentle stretching for beginners to more advanced body-conditioning regimes, ELLE offers you a wide range of fitness alternatives.

BODY FORM
SHAPING AND CONDITIONING EXERCISE

Exercise is essential for the well-being of both body and mind. Physiologically, we need exercise to maintain a healthy, properly functioning body. Psychologically, exercise has many benefits. Current research has revealed that physical activity triggers the release of natural, pleasure-enhancing chemicals from the brain. Endorphins, which are produced by the pituitary gland, and encephalines, which occur in the spinal fluid and brain, are both natural painkillers, similar to opiates like morphine.

These substances are produced by interrelated physical and mental processes, in particular exercise, although acupuncture and electrical stimulation of the brain and skin also appear to trigger their production. When we exercise, we often experience a natural 'high' which makes us feel happier and more energetic. Leading experts on depression advise their patients to exercise regularly in order to increase the production of these pleasure-inducing chemicals.

The body needs regular and varied exercise in order to keep muscles, joints, tendons and ligaments strong, supple and flexible. A fit body can be gauged through a number of basic requirements – the flexibility of muscles and joints; body composition; cardio-respiratory performance; overall strength; and individual muscle endurance. Different types of exercise fulfil specific requirements, so it is important to try to encompass a number of activities in order to maintain overall fitness. For example, jogging, running and fast walking are all aerobic and therefore build up the cardio-respiratory stamina, whereas yoga or stretching will work on muscle tone and flexibility rather than cardiovascular fitness.

Combining two or three types of exercise is the best insurance for maximum health and fitness. If you do a particular exercise routine each day, combine it with a fast-paced walk or a half-hour swim to improve stamina and aerobic capacity. If you run or jog, ensure that you include gentle stretching or weight training to improve strength and flexibility.

Whatever exercise programme you choose, stick to it. Nothing works better, where exercise is concerned, than dedication. Try to put aside at least half an hour each day or every other day for your fitness programme. Once you have mastered a particular exercise regime, it is important to vary the order in which you do the exercises. This will not only ensure that you don't get bored but that your joints and muscles are receiving a different range of movements.

CARDIOVASCULAR AND RESPIRATORY FITNESS

A healthy body depends on healthy cardiovascular and respiratory systems. These consist of the heart, lungs and arteries and it is important to maintain these in order to achieve your optimum fitness level. Aerobic exercise – that is, exercise that involves taking in oxygen – is the best way to improve your cardiovascular fitness levels.

However, that does not mean that you have to work out to music or to 'go for the burn'. Swimming, brisk walking, dancing, cycling, trampolining and jogging are just a few examples of activities that will help you to build up stamina and improve the condition of your heart, lungs and blood circulation. The added benefit of this type of exercise is that it helps to stimulate the metabolism, so creating energy from fats and carbohydrates in the body to work the muscles. Fats can only be broken down in the presence of oxygen, so aerobic exercise is essential for those who want to control their body weight. To achieve the best results, it's essential to do at least 30 minutes of aerobic activity three times a week. You also need to calculate your "target zone" or aerobic heart rate range (see page 29). The range gives you the number of times that your heart should beat per minute while exercising aerobically. This number is about 60–80 per cent of your heart's maximum capacity. Exceeding your range can be detrimental to your health, while working below your range means that you are not getting full benefit from the exercise. You should always avoid working above the upper range of your target zone. If you suffer from any heart disease, seek medical advice and never exceed 70 per cent of your maximum heart rate.

When you are working out, listen to your body signs. The safest and most effective way to gain fitness is to adapt your chosen exercise to your pulse rate and maintain a gradual build-up. Start out slowly and work your way up to your peak target. The fitter you get, the more efficiently your heart will work. Your resting heart rate should decrease as your heart gets stronger and so does not have to work as hard.

FINDING YOUR TARGET ZONE

The Korvonen method allows you to calculate your range accurately:

STEPS	EXAMPLE	YOUR RANGE
1. Clinically determined Maximum Heart Rate (220)	220	
2. Subtract your age	30 / 190	
3. Your maximum heart rate	190	
4. Subtract your resting heart rate (take this on rising in the morning)	70 / 120	
5. Multiply this number by .6 and .8 – you want to work out 60% and 80% of your heart's maximum capacity	120 / x.6 / 72	120 / x.8 / 96
6. Add on your resting heart rate	72 / +70 / 142	96 / +70 / 166
7. This is your target heart range for 1 min.	142	166
8. Divide by 6	÷6	÷6
9. Your target heart range for 10 seconds	23	27 beats

TAKING YOUR PULSE

To ensure that you are working at your target heart range, you have to count your pulse beats. Lightly place your index and middle fingers of one hand at the wrist, on the side where your thumb is – this is the radial artery. Once you have found your pulse, keep exercising until you are ready to count the beats. Start counting your pulse beats as soon as you stop moving, starting with zero, and time the pulse for 10 seconds. Multiply by 6 to find your heart rate for one minute or compare your goal target heart range for 10 seconds. Then adjust your exercise to a higher, lower or continued energy level to stay within your target zone.

PACE YOURSELF

By working harder, you are not necessarily working more efficiently. If you are exercising above your target zone, then you start to exercise anaerobically – or without oxygen. This means that your heart and muscles are not getting sufficient oxygen to function correctly. When you do this, you are slowing down your body's fat-burning process, and allowing it to burn more carbohydrates or glu-

Swimming is one of the best forms of exercise, building stamina and cardiovascular fitness.

cose and, eventually, muscle mass. By exercising too hard, you also over-stress your muscles and lose lean muscle mass.

Steady and continual aerobic exercise improves fitness and produces the heart and muscle enzyme changes that are essential to speed up your metabolism. You actually lose fitness by over-exercising and over-exerting yourself. However, if you exercise at a level of intensity that you can sustain for over 20 minutes, you will improve your fitness level. This should improve your energy levels and help to promote correct sleeping patterns.

To maintain your fitness level, you need to work out at least three times a week for 20 minutes, keeping continuously within your target zone. While to improve your fitness, you have to work out four to six times a week for 20 minutes in your range. Give your body one day a week to rest, rebuild and re-energise. You should still do gentle stretching exercises or yoga when you are resting.

POSTURE

Without good posture, no amount of exercise will improve your body shape. Perfect posture plays a fundamental role in determining how you both look and feel. When the body is correctly aligned, it forms a well-balanced and proportioned silhouette. But if tension is allowed to build up in the muscles and connective tissues, the fine body balance is lost. Not only does a rigid or sagging body look unattractive, it also lacks vitality and is prone to minor health complaints such as cellulite, poor circulation, indigestion and headaches.

Realigning the body involves much more than simply making a conscious effort to stand up straight. The origins of twists and distortions are often deeply rooted in the past.

Many of the causes of poor posture are linked to childhood and adolescence, when we are so self-conscious that we stoop, slump and slouch to hide our developing bodies. In later life, the body tends to mould itself to the position most frequently adopted during work or play. Those who spend day after day bent over a desk begin to carry their hunched shoulders around with them. The bowed legs of the keen horse-rider are a classic sign of physical adaptation.

When it is forced to adopt certain attitudes for long periods of time, the body tries to make them as comfortable as possible. To do this, layers of connective tissue, which cover muscles like a supportive stocking, start sticking together. This lends extra support to strained muscles but, at the same time, fixes the body into its new distorted shape. Continual movement helps to keep the connective tissue pliable and prevents such patterns becoming deeply ingrained. Inactivity encourages rigidity; joints become stiffer and muscles lose some of their flexibility.

PUTTING ON THE PRESSURE

In the forties, Ida Rolf, doctor of physiology and biochemistry and a student of yoga, proposed a method, which combined her fields of knowledge, for releasing the body from postural problems. She realised that, before the body could be rebalanced, the bones and muscles had to be free to readopt their natural positions. This meant the constricting connective tissue had to be manipulated to make it pliable and yielding once again. She developed a technique in which thumbs, knuckles and elbows were employed to work not only on the body surface but also on the deeper layers of tissue.

This process is now known as Rolfing – though Rolf herself termed it 'structural integration' or 'postural release'. Rolf visualised the body as a series of segments, stacked one on top of another. When neatly arranged, a straight line can be drawn through the ear, centre of the shoulder, hip, knee and ankle, showing that the body is perfectly balanced.

This structure (she preferred the term to 'posture') works best for the body. The ribcage can expand to capacity. Blood flows freely round the body, unimpeded by tense, restrictive muscles, and wastes are whisked away from the tissues. This means that organs and muscles can work at an optimum level.

When, because of bad habits, certain segments drift out of line, the body takes on unflattering contours. Prolonged tension in the fixed muscles leads to a build-up of wastes, such as the fatigue chemical, lactic acid. This makes the muscles stiff and sore. Tight muscles also tug on the bones to which they are attached. In due course, the body becomes plagued with all sorts of aches and pains.

As any dancer is aware, feelings and emotions are expressed by the attitude of the body. When a person is sad, the head falls forward, the back

becomes rounded, the shoulders are hunched and the chest caves in.

Frederick Alexander, an actor and dramatist, discovered that when he became anxious – as he invariably did before going on stage – he drew his head back and down into his chest. This interfered with his breathing and voice production, sometimes forcing him to abandon certain performances. Once he became aware of this physical response to anxiety, Alexander tried to do something about it, but without much success.

Watching himself in a mirror, he realised why. Even when he felt he was standing properly, his reflection revealed that he was actually quite out of line. Without looking he couldn't judge whether he was using his body to stand correctly or not. After watching the fluid movements of children and primitive peoples, Alexander realised what many people were lacking and went on to develop his technique, which was to offer, to those who'd lost the instinct, a means of re-discovering what it feels like to stand, sit and move correctly, or 'naturally'.

Alexander's method also teaches ways of preventing emotions interfering with the correct use and position of the body. Much emphasis is placed on the region at the base of the neck, for passing through it are nerve fibres that transmit information about the state of the body's muscles and joints to the brain. When muscles in this area become excessively tense, as they do at times of great fear and anxiety, we begin to lose touch with our bodies.

MUSCLE POWER

In 1881, a gymnast, Joseph Pilates, devised a remedial form of exercise, akin to physiotherapy, for rebalancing the body. He was strongly against what he referred to as unnatural exercise – forcing the body into strained positions and pushing it to repeat the same movement over and over again to the point of exhaustion. He realised that such activity could create and reinforce postural problems. Pilates felt that simple movements, carried out in a precise way, were the most effective.

His exercises are designed to isolate weak, under-used muscles and to prevent the stronger ones from coming to their rescue. Each movement is accompanied by rhythmic breathing to encourage tension release and to avoid build-up of waste in the muscles. Much emphasis is placed on

strengthening the stomach muscles, which help to hold the pelvis in place and stop the lower back arching. When the stomach is firm and flat, standing straight comes naturally. Other muscle groups that are often weak and are implicated in poor alignment are those of the inner thighs, the backs of the thighs, and the upper back (around the shoulder blades). It is here, too, that fat cells tend to accumulate in many people. (For the Pilates workout, see pages 37–39.)

Hellerwork is another form of bodywork that encourages constant awareness of alignment when sitting, standing and moving about. Devised by therapist Joseph Heller, who started teaching the method in California in 1978, Hellerwork is a synthesis of different schools of bodywork and, like Rolfing, it involves manipulation of the connective tissue to release tension and so to allow the body to fall back into line.

'A well-balanced pelvis is central to good structure,' points out Roger Golten, who was taught by Heller and is one of the few Hellerworkers practising in this country. 'When the pelvis is tilted backwards, the spine arches and the stomach falls forwards, which makes it look more rotund than it actually is. Visualisation techniques are very helpful. Think of the pelvis as a bowl that's filled to the brim with water. It is important to keep the bowl balanced at all times to prevent the water from spilling over the edge.' Place your hand on the lower back to check it is not curved when you think the pelvis bowl is level.

If your body is prone to slouching, imagine that the crown of the head is connected to a helium balloon, which is trying to pull you up to the sky. This will help you to lift the chest for fuller and easier breathing and, at the same time, lengthens the abdomen, making the body look much slimmer. If the chest is well balanced over the pelvis when you are standing, you can see your ankles.

ELLE'S BODY-SHAPING AND BODY-CONDITIONING EXERCISES

The following exercise programmes have been devised by expert exercise instructors. Choose a programme that is best suited to your particular lifestyle and that you can adapt to fit into your daily routine. They all have specific benefits, designed to reshape, realign, revive energy levels, or strengthen the body.

BENEFITS OF REGULAR EXERCISE

● It raises the metabolic rate so that the cells of the body burn oxygen in a more efficient way. This encourages more efficient use of nutrients derived from food and increases the rate at which energy is released from food. It also provokes better elimination of waste and by-products.

● It stimulates the digestive system by increasing intestinal peristalsis – the rhythmic movement of the intestines – which is essential for digestion, absorption of vitamins and minerals, and excretion of waste.

● It helps to stabilise blood sugar levels. This is due to the fact that exercised muscles burn more fat rather than carbohydrates – so they don't take as much sugar from the blood.

● It improves the condition of the heart, lungs and blood circulation. In turn, this helps to prevent cardiovascular disease; boosts the immune system; and increases the lung capacity, which, in turn, heightens the body's oxygen intake and improves our energy levels.

● It helps to alleviate depression, stress and fatigue by boosting the production of therapeutic chemicals in the brain. It can also help to regulate sleep patterns in response to the release of another chemical called serotonin, which aids relaxation.

STRETCH EXERCISES TO FIRM, TONE AND STRENGTHEN

Working women lead demanding lives. We need boundless energy and inner strength just to stay on top. It helps, of course, to be fit. Yet frantic pursuit of this quality often does more harm than it does good.

But exercise doesn't have to be gruelling to improve your strength and stamina. Slow stretching improves both flexibility and strength, in addition to helping to firm and tone the body. These exercises are designed to achieve suppleness, eliminate tension, and firm up muscle tone.

Simple stretch movements build strong muscles, too. Strength comes from holding the stretched position. When you perform the exercise properly, muscles may actually shudder because they are working hard. Stretching firms and lengthens the muscles, making them slender and streamlined. Performed regularly and correctly, they can smooth the way in coping with life's pressures, as well as promoting a sleeker, more supple body.

Stretching works by increasing flexibility, especially of the spine, which houses the central nervous system and its connections to every part of the body. When the spine is pulled out of line by tense muscles, health and vitality suffer as well as posture. It is often a better form of exercise than fast, repetitive exercises. The latter work muscles when they are contracted, and often until they become saturated with their own wastes. That builds on existing tension, leaving the muscles feeling stiff, sore and unattractively bulky. Tense muscles interfere with the free flow of blood around the body and contribute to postural problems.

Stretching, on the other hand, makes muscles relax and, in so doing, improves circulation and allows waste to leave the tissues. This makes it a potent weapon against cellulite.

The physical aspect of stretching also has profound psychological benefits. The link between emotional tension and muscle tightness is well known. Gently lengthening the muscles helps to flush out such tension. Nothing seems to work quite like it for discharging stress which, if left bottled up, contributes to fatigue and other problems.

Top exercise teacher Pemma Fox, whose background is in yoga, ballet and orthopaedic movement, is known for her workouts designed to develop body control. This control is not only physical, she maintains, but manifests itself as an inner strength and stamina, which helps you to cope better with life's ups and downs.

Stretch plays an important role in her exercises, which are performed slowly and precisely. If done four or five times a week, they will guarantee a sleeker, fitter, more supple body.

WORK YOUR WAY TO FITNESS WITH THE 10-WAY STRETCH

Good posture is vital, but it only comes with practice. At first, you may feel some discomfort from your new position. It will help if you concentrate on elongating as you inhale, and work into balance as you exhale. Think tall!

1. POSTURE

1 Stand with your legs hip width apart, feet and knees facing forwards. Balance the weight evenly between the heels and balls of the feet, not allowing ankles or arches to roll in or out. To ensure that this is not happening, lift the toes off the ground to align, then place them down again.
2 Don't lock or bend knees. Keep them relaxed and imagine that you are raising the kneecaps without moving them.
3 Exhale and pull navel into the spine, tucking the pelvis under (pubic bone comes forward) and lessening the arch in the back. Draw the cheeks of the bottom in towards each other.
4 Inhale and elongate your ribcage, pulling it out of the waist. Exhale as the pelvis comes into balance. Do not allow the chest to be pushed forwards.
5 Inhale; as you exhale, rotate shoulders in a backward and downward movement towards the middle of the back.

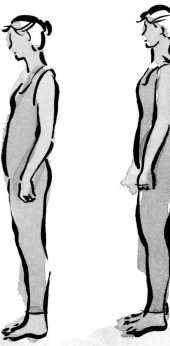

6 Keep the back of the neck lengthened. Try to make your head touch an imaginary hand that is being held one inch above the top of your head.

7 The weight of the entire body should be evenly distributed between the heels and balls of the feet. When you feel this, relax your bottom but do not lose the lift you feel throughout the body.

2. NECK STRETCH

1 Stand in perfect posture. Keep shoulders down as far away from ears as possible. Drop chin forwards slightly. Inhale and, as you exhale, lengthen your neck, then take your ear down to one shoulder and hold for five seconds, making sure that the opposite shoulder does not lift up. It helps consciously to draw the elbows down to keep the shoulders still. Repeat twice on each side.
2 Start as above, and turn head to one side to look as far behind you as possible. Return to centre, then turn to the opposite side. Again, be conscious of keeping the shoulders down by drawing the elbows downwards. Hold for 10 seconds on each side. Repeat twice.

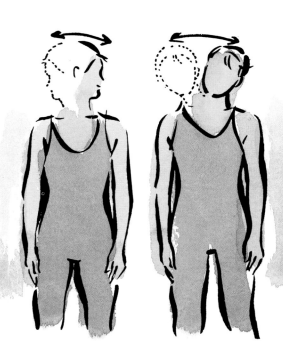

3. UNDERARM STRETCH

1 Stand in perfect posture, feet slightly apart. Drop the head slightly forwards. Take left arm up behind it. Slightly bend the elbow.
2 Inhale and, as you exhale, pull on the arm with the right hand, stretching gradually until you feel a comfortable stretch along the underarm. Hold for 10–15 seconds.
3 Aim to place the left hand on the right shoulder blade. Inhale and, as you exhale, change the line of pull gently downwards, towards the shoulder blades. Hold for 10–15 seconds. Change arms and repeat the movement.

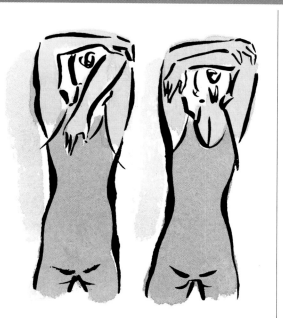

4. SHOULDER BLADES STRETCH

1 Stand in perfect posture, feet hip width apart. Interlock hands above head, keeping the elbows bent.
2 Inhale, pull navel into the spine. Exhale and slowly take elbows back behind head to the left, centre and right before bringing them in front of you (create a circle).
3 Keep shoulders down throughout. Don't involve the head or upper body in the movement.
4 Repeat the circles three times in each direction.

5. SHOULDERS/ SHOULDER BLADES

1 Stand in perfect posture, feet hip width apart. Hold arms at shoulder height in front of you, palms facing.
2 As you exhale, keep arms at shoulder level and slowly take them backwards, making sure that you extend your fingers and palms to their limits. Use only your arms and shoulders to make the movement. Do not involve your head and neck.
3 Keep head and body steady by pulling navel into the spine and letting your shoulders do all the work. Don't lean forwards or lift your shoulders, as the exercise will not be so effective. Hold for five seconds. Repeat the movement several times.

knee is relaxed. It must not be locked tight.
2 Move bent leg forwards without raising hip. Try not to hang on to the chair for support.
3 Inhale and lift your rib cage upwards. As you exhale, pull navel into spine and tilt the tail bone forwards. The pubic bone should line up with the hips.
4 Inhale, keeping the lift in the rib cage. As you exhale, shrug shoulders back, squeezing the shoulder blades together. Remember to keep the tail bone tucked under the whole time.
5 Inhale and keep lifting the rib cage, with navel pulled in. Without releasing tilted tail bone, exhale and draw leg backwards to line up the thighs. Your arm will straighten and you will feel an upward stretch in the chest and a downward stretch in the front of the thigh. Don't bounce the leg backwards, but hold the position just until you feel comfortable, then release. Change legs and repeat.

6. FRONT THIGH STRETCH

1 Holding on to the back of a chair, stand on one leg and grasp the ankle (not the arch) of the other foot with your hand. Ensure that the foot of the standing leg faces forwards and that the

7. CHEST AND SPINE STRETCH

1 Stand about an arm's length away from a wall, feet hip width apart, legs and feet facing forwards.
2 Raise and place both arms above you on the wall, shoulder width apart. Ensure palms and fingers are stretched to their limits and that the elbows are locked straight.
3 Inhale, pull navel into the spine, tilt pelvis forwards (to keep the stress off the small of the back). As you exhale, lift the chest forwards and upwards towards the wall, at the same time drawing the shoulder blades together and down at the back (chest and breastbone lifting, shoulder blades dropping).
4 Keep body in a straight slant by keeping the pelvis firm and not allowing the bottom to stick out, otherwise you'll put stress on your back. You'll feel the chest opening up and spine lengthening, as well as a stretch in the arms and shoulders. Try holding for 15 seconds, initially, then build up to 30.

STRETCH

8. SPINAL STRETCH

1 Kneel on all fours, legs forming a straight line with the hips and hands (palms down, fingers flat and forwards), which should be placed slightly forward of the shoulders. Legs should be hip width and arms shoulder width apart. The back should be relaxed.

2 Inhale. Exhale, pull navel into the spine and arch back as high as possible, relaxing the head and back of the neck. Press shoulders down towards the shoulder blades. Hold this stretch for five to 10 seconds. Relax. Repeat three times.

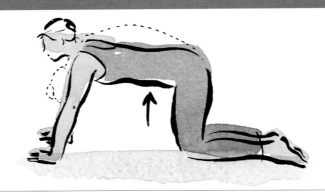

9. COMPLETE SIDE STRETCH

1 Imagine an imaginary line painted down one side of your body, from wrist to underarm, past the side of the knee and on to the ankle.

2 Lie sideways on an exercise mat or thick blanket directly on this line (see below), lengthening the body until the lower hip bone is parallel with the top. Extend the arms over and under the head, just behind the ears. The head should not drop forwards.

3 Bend the lower leg for balance at a 40° angle to the body, aligning the knee and heel. Ensure that the upper body and shoulders have not been allowed to drop forwards of the hips, otherwise the back will become curved.

4 Grasp the top arm 7.5 cm (3 inches) above the wrist with the lower hand. Flex the foot of the top leg until the heel is square with the knee, the toes and knees facing forwards. Tilt the pelvis to ensure that the small of the back is kept flat.

5 Inhale. Exhale, hold the tilt, pull navel firmly into spine and lift the top leg off the ground in a straight line with (and no higher than) the hip. Ensure the foot has not moved forwards and the hips have remained steady. The spine should be one straight line from the nape of the neck to the tail bone, and aligned with the back of the head and the heel of the foot.

6 Inhale. Exhale, keeping navel pulled in, and lift rib cage towards the shoulders. Lengthen the hip and leg in the opposite direction (pushing with a firm heel) until you feel the waist open up. Concentrate on lengthening the chest upwards instead of pulling on shoulder socket with the arm.

7 Once the stretch feels comfortable, relax the foot and hold the position for 10–15 seconds. Change over to the other side. Repeat the movement one more time.

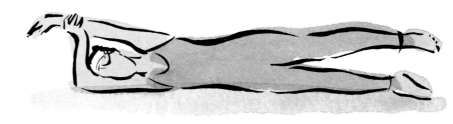

10. HAMSTRING AND TENDON STRETCH

1 Kneel on all fours, legs hip width apart, with the knees and feet forming a straight line.

2 Bring up one leg in front of the hip, ensuring that the knee is placed over the heel.

3 Align hip bones and shoulders so the hips and upper body face forwards. Curl the toes of the back leg under the foot, so the heel and knee form a straight line.

4 Place both hands (shoulders square) on either side of the front foot, shoulder width apart.

5 Inhale. As you exhale, pull navel into the spine and shrug the shoulders back away from the ears, pulling the chest forwards, and raise the back knee off the ground. Try to open the back of the knee by pressing the heel away from you. Do not bounce the hips. You must keep the back in a straight slant by not allowing the hips to drag down. (If you do, the hip of the stretched leg will hang down, throwing your weight off balance, twisting the groin and pinching the lower back.) If done correctly, this position should feel quite comfortable. Hold for 10–15 seconds (building up) and then gently place the knee back on the ground, still keeping the navel pulled into the spine.

6 Flatten back foot. Inhale, keep the navel pulled in and, without altering the alignment of the legs, shoulders and arms, exhale and move your hips backwards (hip bones parallel) until they are directly over the back knee. Your front leg will extend and hands remain on floor.

7 Inhale. Exhale, pull navel in, align hips and balance your weight evenly. Lengthen the spine and take your chest as far forwards towards the front leg as is comfortable, keeping shoulders pressed back from the ears. (Any stress felt on the back means either that your hips are uneven or that you have dropped too far forwards.) The stretch in the front hamstring should be quite comfortable. (If you feel pins and needles or any stress, this means the legs have not been sufficiently warmed up or that you are over-stretching.)

8 Hold the stretch for 10–15 seconds, then centre the body until both knees are bent. Place the front leg under the body and relax on the floor, bottom resting on heels and head on arms. Change legs and repeat the movement.

PILATES-BASED PROGRAMME EXERCISES TO REALIGN THE BODY

The Pilates-based exercise philosophy is that good posture and even muscle tone are the two basic requirements necessary for maximum health.

Pilates-based exercise teacher, Christina Hocking, has devised a revitalising body programme exclusively for ELLE. Follow these simple but effective exercises and you will improve your posture, increase your energy levels, relax your mind and even reshape your body within a matter of weeks.

Perfect posture is the basis for a super-fit and vital body and, regardless of how much we exercise and diet, it is unlikely that our bodies will function correctly if our posture is poor. Bad posture leads to a number of health problems, not least lack of energy, bad circulation, tension, back pain and fatigue. A poorly aligned skeleton causes muscle imbalance and an uneven distribution of muscle tone.

The exercises work by redressing muscle balance. For example, tension in a muscle is the result of constant overwork. This tension can only be released if the muscles are rebalanced. The Pilates method does this by stimulating the muscle that is opposite the overworked one, thereby re-establishing correct balance and releasing built-up tension. Most of us have weak stomach muscles, for example, which put pressure on our back muscles to do more work, often leading to backache and tension.

Christina Hocking believes that the system is essential for maintaining optimum health because it rebalances both mind and body. 'The Pilates system corrects bad posture and poor muscle tone, using a series of highly controlled physical exercises. Because the exercises demand a high level of concentration, it is also an excellent means of releasing both physical and mental tension.'

Hocking's methods are derived from the method originated by Joseph Pilates, who devised the Pilates system over 60 years ago. His aim was to increase body awareness and to integrate body and mind by means of controlled movements. The method's goal is to create a unity of mind and body so that you can move with grace, balance and freedom without thinking about it. The exercises are aimed at strengthening and rebalancing the muscles, especially in the centre of the body, from the bottom of your ribcage to just above the hips. Pilates referred to this area as the body's 'powerhouse'. Hocking has combined these essential elements with her own ideas to create effective, body-controlling movements, which really do revitalise and revive body and soul.

Perfect posture is the key to vitality and reshaping your body. Realignment improves not only your strength, but also your silhouette.

Hocking, a dancer, choreographer and movement teacher, has been teaching Pilates-based exercise for over eight years. Her classes are always well attended by both professional dancers and those who want to reshape and realign their body with the successful system. Another bonus with the exercises is that they never leave you tired or drained. 'If they do, then you are doing them incorrectly,' says Hocking. 'Most people judge an exercise class by how much they sweat, how tired they feel afterwards or how much their muscles ache. Pilates-based techniques work your body gently but super-effectively, without unnecessary pain.'

PILATES-BASED PROGRAMME EXERCISES TO REALIGN THE BODY

Christina Hocking has designed 10 rebalancing exercises, which illustrate the basic principles of Pilates-based training. Read the following points carefully before embarking on the programme.

● The exercises do not need to be repeated more than the stated number of times. The aim is to concentrate fully on each exercise, to control the movement and to breathe correctly.
● Never rush the movements. Keep a slow, even pace.
● Never tense up or over-control the muscles while exercising. If you become aware of tension, relax the muscle just enough to hold the position without strain.
● Read the instructions to each exercise carefully. Take note of important points, such as pulling in

the stomach muscles, keeping the back or spine flat on the floor, keeping the neck and back stretched, flexing or pointing your feet and relaxing your shoulders. All these are essential if you are to reap the maximum benefits from the system.
● Never exercise directly on the floor. Always use a mat, a rug or a thick towel to prevent injury to the spine.
● Wear comfortable, non-restrictive clothing, which allows freedom of movement.
● Exercise in front of a mirror, if possible, so that you can check that your posture is correct.
● If you have had any serious injury to your neck or spine, or you have problems with back or neck pain, consult a doctor before embarking on the programme. The movements are subtle but deep-reaching.

3. ARM CIRCLES

1 Lie on floor, knees bent, feet flat on floor and arms resting by your side. Inhale.
2 Exhale, turn your palms up and make circular movements with your arms, keeping them stretched out straight and in contact with the floor until they meet behind your head. Keep your back and feet flat on the floor, trying to keep your hips and pelvis as still as possible. Inhale and return to the starting position. Repeat the circles 10 times, at a slow and even pace.

1. CURLING THE SPINE

1 Sit bolt upright, with a straight back and neck. Keep legs straight out in front of you, with toes pointed forwards and backs of knees in contact with floor. Stretch arms out in front of you at shoulder level, palms facing down. Keep shoulders relaxed and neck long. Inhale.
2 As you exhale, pull in your stomach towards your spine, drop your head, aiming your nose towards your navel without forcing your chin down, and round your spine. Don't grip with your buttocks. It may help if you imagine your body is making a 'C' shape.
Note: the lower section of

the spine often resists this stretch, making you lean backwards. With practice,

you will be able to do this exercise without leaning back so much. Hold for a count of five, release and return to starting position. Inhale. Repeat five times.

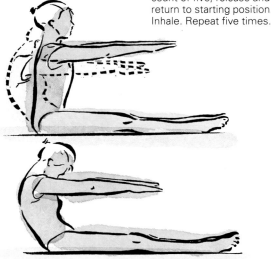

4. BACK STRETCH

1 This exercise helps to work the abdominal muscles correctly and stretches the muscles of the lower back. It also helps to release tension in the lower spine.
2 Exhale and curl forwards, elbows pulling in as you

reach towards your knees. Keep the stomach flat, navel pulled in to the spine.
3 Reach forwards with arms and raise one knee towards your body, placing hands lightly on the knee to increase the stretch. Release and exhale, returning to the starting position. Repeat five times on each side.

2. PARALLEL ARM REACHES

Exercises 2 and 3 improve the blood circulation to the muscles of the back, help to release tension, improve the shoulder line and help to stretch out the lower back.
1 Lie on floor, with neck and back stretched out, knees bent and feet flat on floor. Stretch arms out on floor, in a 'V' shape a few inches away from the hips, and with palms down. Pull in your stomach towards the spine and keep knees and feet together.
2 Reach up to the ceiling, palms facing away from you, arms straight.
3 Reach one arm down by your side, palm down, while reaching behind your head with the opposite

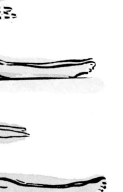

arm, palm up, so that you create a rowing movement. Inhale as you bring your arms back to the centre and exhale as you stretch them in opposition.
Note: don't tilt the pelvis or

arch the back during this exercise. Always ensure that your back is flat on the floor and that your stomach muscles are pulled in and up towards the ribs.

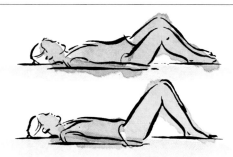

5. HIP ROLLS

This improves shoulder alignment, the tone of the abdominal muscles and helps to stretch the back muscles and joints, thereby reducing muscle spasm.
1 Lie on floor, back flat, knees and feet together, knees bent, arms out to side, palms down. Pull stomach in and inhale.
2 As you exhale, let your

legs fall to one side, feeling a stretch along your opposite side. Make sure you keep knees and feet together and parallel. Don't let knees drop to the ground. Try to keep ribs and hips in contact with the floor. Inhale and go back to the starting position.
3 Repeat stretch to the other side. Repeat five times to each side.

6. DEVELOPPES

This exercise releases tension in the backs of the legs and works the abdominal muscles.
1 Assume the same starting position as in 5.
2 Bring one knee up to chest at an angle of 90°.
3 Keeping the tail bone down, the stomach flat and pulled in, raise the leg, stretching it towards the ceiling with foot flexed.
4 Lower the leg to the floor, keeping stomach pulled in and spine flat against floor.
5 Place leg on floor, foot flexed.
6 Bring leg back to starting position and repeat five times with each leg.

7. CAT STRETCH

This stretches the spine and releases accumulated tension in the back.
1 Kneel on floor with knees directly under hips and hands under shoulders. Keep arms straight and elbow joints facing outwards. Legs should be hip distance apart. Keep back flat and stomach pulled in.

2 Exhale and round back, letting head drop down, chin towards chest, and feeling a stretch along the spine. Hold for a count of five and release. Repeat five to 10 times.

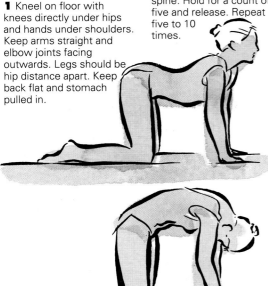

8. SINGLE LEG STRETCH

This is the ultimate stomach exercise, which balances tone between the back and stomach muscles.
1 Lie on floor, knees bent and with one leg pulled towards you, hands resting lightly on the knee but not gripping. Keep your spine flat on the floor and stomach pulled in.
2 Curl forwards, pulling in with abdominal muscles and ensuring that the lower back is still touching the floor.
3 Exhaling, stretch the opposite leg away from you, holding it straight and feeling a stretch along the whole leg. Inhale and return to position 2. Exhale, then repeat the stretch with the

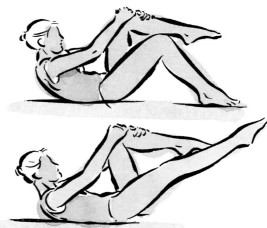

other leg. Repeat five times with each leg. Note: you may experience some neck strain initially. This is due to the back muscles being stronger than the stomach muscles. As the stomach muscles become stronger and the back more flexible, the neck strain will lessen. If you feel too much strain, do fewer repetitions.

9. ROLL DOWN

This exercise strengthens the abdominal muscles and releases tension in the back.
1 Stand upright, chest and shoulders open and relaxed. Let arms fall by sides, keep hips straight, and legs and feet parallel and slightly apart. Keep the stomach pulled in and the back straight.
2 Pulling in the stomach muscles, exhale and curl down, chin to chest, letting the knees bend and the arms hang freely. Curl down until the spine is fully curved.

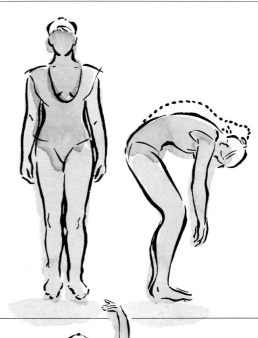

10. SITTING SIDE STRETCH

This exercise opens the chest and stretches the sides and waist.
1 Sit on the floor, knees bent and legs open, soles of feet together. If necessary, use a wall or any vertical surface to support the back and prevent you from slumping. Keep the back straight and elongated, and the stomach pulled in. Let the arms rest gently on the knees, palms down.
2 Raise one arm above head, with elbow lifted forwards. Keep legs relaxed and hips in contact with the floor.

3 and **4** Using the opposite arm to support you, stretch over your head, reaching out to the side as far as possible, feeling a stretch along your side. Return to position 2 and repeat four times. Repeat the stretch five times on the other side.

REVITALISE EXERCISES TO TONE AND STRENGTHEN AND TO IMPROVE CARDIOVASCULAR FITNESS

This programme has been devised by Bridget Woods in conjunction with Melanie Stapes, a trained sports physiologist. It is in two sections.

Part 1 comprises eight exercises to tone and strengthen muscles all over the body. Each week the exercises become harder and may involve weights, which will simply speed up the results. Perform them at least every other day and follow our progress chart opposite.

Part 2 is an aerobic programme. Vigorous exercise raises the metabolic rate while it is being performed and may also, in the long run, make your body become more efficient at converting calories into energy as opposed to laying them down as fat.

PART ONE
1. EASY PRESS-UPS

Adopt the traditional press-up position with hands shoulder distance apart. Bend your knees so they are hip distance apart and cross ankles. Lean forwards so weight is carried by arms. With the stomach pulled in and back straight, bend your elbows and drop your body as low as possible. Inhale. Then straighten arms and exhale.

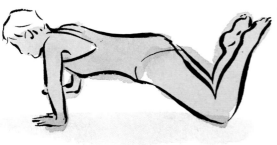

2. FOR THE ARMS

Hold arms out to the sides, at shoulder height and with palms facing forwards. Clench the fists and bend arms so fists are level with the ears. Push the fists forwards and down in a semi-circle, rotating from the elbow joint and resisting the movement, then push back up, still resisting. Keep the upper arms level with the shoulders.

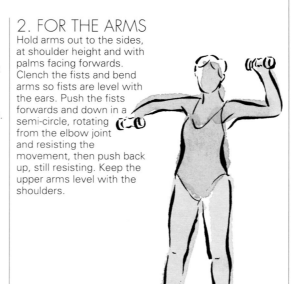

3. WAIST STRETCHES

Stand with legs hip distance apart and knees slightly bent, tucking your bottom under. Drop right hand down the right leg, reaching for the knee, then return to the starting position. Check sideways in a mirror to ensure you don't lean forward. To make the exercise harder, bring the left arm up to the ear and reach up out of the hips as you lean over. Finally, take both arms above the head, clasping wrists or hands. Repeat on the other side.

4. STOMACH STRENGTHENERS

Sit on the floor with the feet apart, knees bent and arms at sides. Pull the stomach in and roll down slowly until the whole back lies flat on floor. Keep the head lifted slightly. Roll back up for a count of eight, breathing out, and down for a count of eight, breathing in. To make it harder, cross arms in front of your chest and, finally, behind your head.

5. TILTS FOR STOMACH, HIPS AND THIGHS

Kneel on the floor with knees hip distance apart, pull in the stomach and hold your arms out straight in front of you at shoulder height. Lean backwards, keeping your back straight, for a count of eight, then come back to centre for a count of eight.

YOUR EXERCISE PROGRESS CHART

EXERCISE 1
WEEK ONE
10 press-ups, legs bent
WEEK TWO
20 press-ups, legs bent
WEEK THREE
10 with legs bent, five with legs straight
WEEK FOUR
Three groups of five press-ups, legs straight, with pause in between

EXERCISE 2
WEEK ONE
20 arm pushes
WEEK TWO
10 with 1 kg (2 lb) weights in each hand
WEEK THREE
20 with weights
WEEK FOUR
20 with weights

EXERCISE 3
WEEK ONE
20 waist stretches to each side
WEEK TWO
20 to each side with one arm reaching above head
WEEK THREE
20 to each side with both arms above head
WEEK FOUR
20 with arms above head and holding 1 kg (2 lb) weights in each hand

EXERCISE 4
WEEK ONE
20 stomach strengtheners with hands at sides
WEEK TWO
20 with arms crossed at the chest
WEEK THREE
20 with hands behind head and elbows pointing forwards
WEEK FOUR
20 with hands behind head and elbows pushing back

EXERCISE 5
WEEK ONE
five lower body tilts
WEEK TWO
10 tilts
WEEK THREE
10 with arms crossed at chest
WEEK FOUR
15 with arms crossed at chest

NB Week four is a maintenance programme to be followed on a regular basis. If it becomes too easy, simply increase the number of repetitions.

6. LEG SPLITS FOR INNER THIGHS

Lie on your back and spread your arms out to the sides, raising legs up in the air. Open your legs sideways, pointing the toes, and then close them again, flexing the feet. Check that your lower back does not arch as you open and close the legs. To make the exercise harder, circle the feet when the legs are stretched out to the sides, and finally add weights to the ankles.

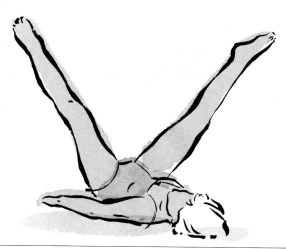

7. LEG KICKS FOR HIPS AND THIGHS

Kneel on all fours with hands and knees hip distance apart. Bend your right leg and lift it to the side, keeping your weight evenly distributed over both hands. Repeat with the other leg. To make the exercise harder, do lifts with the leg straight, and finally add ankle weights.

8. LIFTS FOR THE BOTTOM

Lie on your back with legs bent, feet and knees hip distance apart, and rest hands at the sides. Lift your bottom slightly off the floor and pull stomach in. Squeeze your bottom to raise hips, hold for a count of two and release for a count of two. Repeat. To make the exercise harder, raise one leg up in the air and finally extend it out at a 45° angle in front of you.

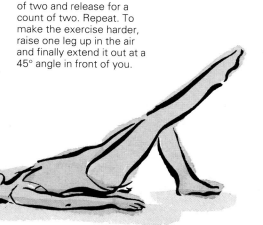

PART TWO

This is the aerobic section

Aerobic exercise is any kind of vigorous but rhythmic activity, such as running, swimming and cycling. If you are unaccustomed to exercising, it may be a good idea to begin this section of exercises on the second week of the diet, otherwise it may place too much strain on the body. If you are already quite fit, begin when you wish.

Aim to do your aerobic exercise three times a week for maximum benefits. Make sure you have the correct footwear before attempting the running part of this programme. A good sports shop will advise on the right kind of shoes for the surface you intend to use. If possible, avoid running on concrete as this can jar the joints and result in back, knee and ankle problems.

RUNNING PROGRAMME

WEEK	PACE	TOTAL TIME
ONE	Jog for three minutes, walk for four, alternately, ending with one minute of jogging	15 minutes
TWO	Jog the whole time at a gentle pace	20 minutes
THREE	Extend your steps so you are running. Come back to a gentle jog if short of breath	25 minutes
FOUR	Run/jog (maintenance)	25–30 minutes

SWIMMING PROGRAMME

WEEK	PACE	TOTAL TIME
ONE	Three slow lengths, three fast lengths	15 minutes
TWO	Three slow lengths, four fast lengths	21 minutes
THREE	Three slow lengths, five fast lengths	25 minutes
FOUR	Two slow lengths, five fast lengths	30 minutes

WALKING PROGRAMME

WEEK	PACE	TOTAL TIME
ONE	Slow, easy pace	15 minutes
TWO	Medium pace	20 minutes
THREE	Medium pace for 15 minutes, fast pace for 10 minutes	25 minutes
FOUR	Medium pace for 10 minutes, fast pace for 15 minutes. 5 minutes to cool down	30 minutes

---

EXERCISE 6
WEEK ONE
20 leg splits
WEEK TWO
20 plus 10 with legs circling clockwise and 10 anti-clockwise
WEEK THREE
As week one, with 1 kg (2 lb) ankle weights
WEEK FOUR
As week two, with 1 kg (2 lb) ankle weights

EXERCISE 7
WEEK ONE
20 leg kicks each leg
WEEK TWO
20 each leg plus 10 with leg stretched each side
WEEK THREE
As week two, with 1 kg (2 lb) ankle weights
WEEK FOUR
Each leg, 20 lifts leg bent, 20 lifts leg straight with ankle weights

EXERCISE 8
WEEK ONE
30 bottom lifts
WEEK TWO
30 plus 10 with one leg stretched to ceiling. Repeat with other leg lifted.
WEEK THREE
30 plus 10 with leg extended forwards. Repeat with other leg.
WEEK FOUR
As week three, with 1 kg (2 lb) weight added to outstretched leg.

BODY SCULPTURE EXERCISES TO RESHAPE BODY CONTOURS

'Dreas Reyneke is exercise instructor to famous names such as Joan Collins, Marie Helvin, Lee Remick and Christopher Lambert. He devised this programme exclusively for ELLE, and maintains that you can reshape your body in fewer than 20 one-hour sessions.

Most people are resigned to their body shape, believing that no amount of exercise will change it enough to make all that effort worthwhile. But in fewer than 20 exercise sessions, it is possible to resculpt your body, re-align your posture and rethink your attitude to exercise.

Since leaving the Ballet Rambert in 1972, 'Dreas Reyneke has dedicated himself to body conditioning – carefully designed exercises that develop specific muscles and help to improve posture and strength. His work has helped dancers, actors and the rich and famous, many of whom he has helped to perfect and recondition. You're quite likely to bump into any one of

his clients on the stairs of the body-conditioning studio in London.

Although Reyneke normally works on a one-to-one basis, he has created a programme suitable for unsupervised use at home. The exercises have two main aims: to improve the mobility and freedom of the body and to bring muscle and joint interaction in line with improved posture. The key, according to Reyneke, is in getting the breathing and posture exercises right.

Reyneke's expertise and reputation make it no surprise that his advice is much sought after and that his classes are both expensive and exclusive. But with ELLE's specially-designed body-conditioning programme, you don't have to attend the classes to benefit – you can improve your body shape at home. Start with the basic exercises and move slowly and gradually through the other levels to ensure maximum benefits.

REMEMBER
● **Read through the exercises before beginning and follow the diagrams carefully.**
● **Master the basic exercises before attempting other levels.**
● **When on more advanced levels, always warm up with the basics.**
● **Work beside a full-length mirror or window, to check your alignment.**
● **Never continue with an exercise if it causes any pain or discomfort.**
● **If you have had any injuries or back pain, you must consult a GP.**

THE BASIC EXERCISES

These should be mastered before attempting the next levels.

1. BASIC BREATHING

1 Practise breathing, using a feather to gauge a slow and even out breath. Exhale steadily over a count of six. Repeat 10 times. Once this is controlled, exhale for eight, then 10. This is the basis of all the exercises.
2 Sit down. This time, as you exhale, straighten the back, pull in stomach and buttock muscles and sit tall, as if rising from the buttocks. Keep feet pressed against floor and thighs against each other.

3 Lie on a flat, firm surface, with knees bent, breathe in and then exhale for a count of six while pressing thighs together and pulling stomach in. Your back should be flat against surface. Point your chin down and relax head and neck.

2. REBOUNDING

This is a good warm-up. Stand on the rebounder and press against a wall with hands. Run on the spot, making sure you lift knees high, with stomach and buttock muscles pulled in. As you exhale, count to six. Continue for one or two minutes. Gradually build up the time, aiming for 10 minutes. As you become tired, the out breath will become irregular and you will begin to inhale more deeply.

3. SIDE STRETCHES

Stand tall, legs apart and feet parallel, arms above head and shoulders down. Leaning slightly forwards to avoid straining lower back, breathe in, stretch sideways and exhale over a count of six. Repeat on other side. Keep hips still and weight evenly distributed over both feet. Repeat 20 times.

4. POSTURAL SQUAT

Stand with legs apart and feet parallel. Keeping back straight, slowly lower into a squat. Rise slowly. Make sure feet are not turning out. Exhale for a count of six as you lower and again as you rise. Keep back vertical, chin pointing downwards and stomach pulled in. Repeat 10 times. Resting against wall, use weight of arms to make small flapping movements towards and away from sides. Turn hands in and out alternately. Repeat 10 times.

5. LEG STRETCH

1 Stand 3 feet from wall. Place hands on wall at shoulder height, parallel to each other. Lean against them while pressing heel of left foot on ground and lifting right heel up. Alternate feet to create a treading motion and repeat 10 times.
2 Step forwards and place weight over front foot. Stretch back leg behind, keeping feet parallel. Press against wall for a count of six. Change legs and repeat 10 times.

6. BACK STRETCH

1 Stand 0.6 m (2 feet) from wall. Lean against it with your spine pulled flat. Keep your head and neck relaxed, looking straight ahead. Exhale, pulling stomach in for a count of six. Repeat 10 times.
2 While exhaling, slide down wall, keeping legs slightly apart and knees parallel. Inhale. Exhale. Slide up to starting position. Repeat 10 times.
3 Breathing out, slowly peel back off wall until you are curved over towards the floor. Exhale. Slowly return to start, vertebra by vertebra. Repeat 10 times.

7. ARM REBOUNDS

1 In standing position, keep legs apart and knees slightly bent. With back resting against wall, use weight of arms to make small flapping movements towards and away from sides. Turn hands in and out alternately. Repeat 10 times.
2 Keeping starting position as before, make large flapping movements with

arms, again alternating hands in and out. Start slowly, ensuring that shoulders are down and neck is stretched. Increase

speed gradually. Once you have mastered these, do them freestanding, keeping back straight and shoulders dropped.

THE SECOND LEVEL

8. POSTURAL CONTROL

Stand close to a high seat. Keep feet wide apart and slightly turned out. Head should be still and tilted slightly downwards. Take a deep breath and, as you exhale, without bending back or moving head, slowly lower your body until seated on the chair edge. Repeat 10 times.

9. STOMACH LIFTS

1 Lie on stomach, with hands flat on floor. This is the starting position.

Exhale, lift stomach and press forearms into floor. Hold for a count of six. Inhale, exhale, repeat 10 times.

CHEST PRESS

2 Lift elbows and press on hands to lift chest, stomach and head, without arching back. Hold for a count of six. Repeat 10 times.

TORSO PUSH-UP

3 From starting position, rise up on to knees, back straight, head down, stomach pulled in. Lower, exhaling over a count of six.

BODY SCULPTURE EXERCISES TO RESHAPE BODY CONTOURS

THE THIRD LEVEL

10. HIP RELEASE

1 Kneel on all fours, with hips behind knees. Lift knee up to chest.
2 Controlling breath and pulling stomach up, slowly raise bent leg to side.
3 Move the raised leg from side to back, keeping it bent with toes pointed. Repeat four times, then reverse the movement. Make sure that the supporting hip and leg are kept still and that you continue to look at the floor. Repeat the exercise with the other leg.

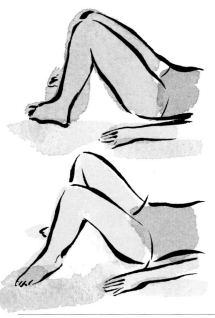

11. INSIDE THIGH STRETCH

1 Lie on back, with arms by your sides, thighs and bottom tightened, legs apart, knees bent and feet turned in. This is the starting position. Pull in stomach, exhale and lengthen back as if you were growing. Press against feet and slowly press knees together to feel inside thigh muscles working. Repeat 10 times.
2 Legs and feet wide apart and turned out, pull stomach down against back. Press sides of feet down. Exhale and push down on feet, keeping small of back against floor and stomach pulled in. Repeat 10 times.

12. BUTTOCK FIRMER

1 From starting position, lift pelvis, tightening buttocks and keeping back straight. Press thighs together and hold for a count of six. Repeat 10 times.
2 With your legs apart, lift your pelvis, tightening buttocks and keeping your feet pressed down. Repeat 10 times.

THE FOURTH LEVEL

13. BODY STRETCH

1 Start as in 10, making sure that hips are behind knees. Lift knee to chest, then stretch leg backwards and lift high with foot flexed. Exhale. Bring leg back to chest and inhale. Repeat four times with each leg.

2 Start as above. Stretch leg backwards and move leg round to side, keeping it at hip height. Hold for a count of three. Stretch leg backwards again, then bring forwards to your chest. Repeat four times each side.

14. INNER THIGH STRENGTH

1 Lie on side, legs together, underneath arm bent and head supported on one hand. Turn bottom leg in, foot upwards to press up against top heel. Lift bottom leg and hold for a count of six, while exhaling. Repeat 10 times on each side.
2 Lie on side with top leg bent over bottom leg and foot pressed flat on floor. Flex other foot upwards and lift leg off mat. Hold for a count of six, while exhaling. Repeat 10 times on each side.

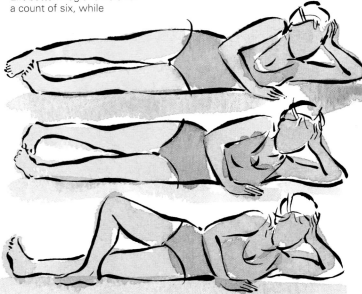

15. ROCKING

Lie on your back with your knees bent and your hands resting on your legs. Sit up slowly, moving hands to knees, and then return to the starting position in a rocking motion. Repeat 10 times to alleviate lower back strain.

16. BACK WINDER

1 Stand upright with your legs apart and feet parallel. Keeping body still but relaxed, swing arms loosely around body in wrapping movement. After eight swings, turn head with swing. After eight more, turn shoulders and finally torso. Keep your waist still at all times.

2 As you swing your left arm round, put your weight on your left foot. Transfer your weight to your right foot as you swing your right arm. Look behind you on each turn. Repeat eight times.

3 Swing arms in front of you above shoulder height from side to side, keeping hips still and stomach pulled in. Repeat eight times, then transfer your weight on to one foot at a time and swing round in a spiral movement from supporting hip. Pull stomach in while you exhale.

THE ADVANCED LEVEL

17. CYCLING

Lie on back, leaning on forearms, head and shoulders up, stomach in. Exhale, bring knee towards chest. Alternate legs. Repeat 20 times to tone stomach.

18. STOMACH TIGHTENER

Sit upright, with your knees bent towards your chest and hands by sides. On exhaling, lift one knee towards chest. Alternate 12 times. Stop if lower back hurts or strains. Then, still sitting, exhale for a count of six. Lift both feet off floor and hold for a count of six. Repeat six times.

19. STOMACH STRENGTHENER

Lie on back, knees bent. Support head with hands. Breathe out slowly and release one hand to reach forwards to opposite knee, while remaining hand supports head as head and neck lift off mat. As you become stronger, take the supporting hand away.

20. OUTER THIGH TONER

Lie on side, hand supporting head and bottom leg bent. Stretch the top leg back, foot flexed and turned downwards. Lift leg up and stretch, holding for a count of six, then lift leg over body to front, holding for a count of six. Take the leg back again, exhale and hold for a count of six. Repeat the whole exercise six times on each side.

21. WAIST TRIMMER

Sit on one buttock, with your knees bent and feet tucked in. Inhale, then exhale slowly and stretch out your legs to the front. Bend and bring them back to the body, still keeping them elevated. Repeat the whole exercise six times on each side.

22. LOWER STOMACH TIGHTENER

Lie on back, knees held at a 90° angle. Exhale, pull stomach in and feel spine stretch. Ankles crossed, slowly straighten legs. Repeat eight times, hanging legs after each breath. Holding legs straight will prevent back strain, but stop if necessary.

CHAPTER THREE

BREATHING AND YOGA

Breathing is essential to our well-being. The very essence of our life force, correct breathing techniques are the basis of many ancient healing philosophies. Yet why is it that westerners have forgotten how to breathe properly? We hold our breath when we are tense and shallow breathe when we are anxious, instead of using our breath to control our emotions. Hand in hand with deep, therapeutic breathing, yoga helps us to tap into our hidden energy resources and promotes both physical and mental relaxation. Not only is it relaxing but it also has a remedial effect on the body, helping to strengthen, stretch, firm and tone the muscles.

AIR WAVES
THE POWER OF BREATH

Air: it's all around us; it's what we breathe. And yet we take it for granted. Few of us actually breathe correctly and, although it's an automatic response, it seems that we have almost forgotten how to do it properly.

While most of us in the western world use only a small percentage of our lung capacity, our counterparts in the East appear to have a higher understanding of the power of breath. It is no wonder, then, that alternative therapists are taking inspiration from these eastern techniques, in order to re-educate our breathing habits to improve body, mind and soul.

Breath has always been synonymous with energy and vitality. The Chinese refer to this invisible life force as *chi,* while in India it's known as *prana,* meaning breath, life, energy and strength. In the East, breath is utilised to its full potential. The Chinese use breath control to enable their bodies to bend and stretch with greater flexibility in their exercise practices, such as *tai chi, aikido* and *karate.* Indian yogis can control their breath so adeptly that they can easily achieve a deep state of relaxation within minutes. In some eastern cultures, breath is even used to reach the *theta* state – the deepest level of meditation.

WHAT IS AIR?

What we actually breathe to keep us alive is a carefully balanced combination of gases. Air is made up of 78 per cent nitrogen, 21 per cent oxygen and .03 per cent carbon dioxide, plus small proportions of inert gases, including helium, argon, xenon, krypton and neon. It also contains water in the form of tiny molecules of humidity absorbed from the rain, mist and clouds.

Unfortunately it also contains an increasing number of environmental pollutants. In addition, air is also subject to ionisation and carries an overall positive or negative electrical charge, which changes with weather or pollution conditions.

Scientists believe that negatively charged air is most beneficial to our mind and body. Many people report feelings of depression and lethargy just before a storm when the air is positively charged and a surge of energy or an increased sense of well-being afterwards, when negative ions abound. Electric ionisers work on this principle, discharging the negative ions that appear to improve our sense of well-being.

BREATHING FOR ENERGY

So why is it that we have so little power over our most important life-support system – when correct breathing can improve our health so dramatically? Continual fatigue, an inability to concentrate and low energy levels can all be treated very simply by proper breathing.

When we breathe, we supply our bodies' cells with oxygen. Not only does this essential nutrient generate energy but, as we exhale, we expel toxic wastes, primarily carbon dioxide, which would otherwise poison our systems. When we don't breathe deeply enough, cells do not obtain the optimum oxygen supply and cannot operate with maximum efficiency. As a result, we feel tired for no apparent reason.

Our emotions also affect our breathing and the way that we breathe can reveal much about our state of mind. In the 1920s, the renowned Viennese psychotherapist, Wilhelm Reich, pioneered work into the link between breath and the emotions. Reich saw breath as the most immediate and intimate connection that he could have with his patient's emotional experiences. He taught his patients to breathe with the whole body and mind and encouraged them to feel 'streamings' – breath-related energy that flowed throughout the body.

Yet it was not until 1969 that the value of his discoveries was fully understood and expanded. Norwegian physiotherapist, Gerda Boyesen, was co-discoverer of a technique of working directly with body-based emotional releases. By monitoring abdominal sounds while her patients 'breathed in their emotions', she discovered that peristaltic, or digestive, sounds reflected an emotional release. The Boyesen technique became known as psychoperistalsis, or psychoperistaltic massage, and served as the foundation for later work, which is now known as bio-dynamic therapy.

According to Boyesen and the ancient eastern breathing experts, short, fast breaths reveal anxiety, anger, fear and other kinds of emotional upset. Fast breathing also signifies pleasure and excitement when combined with a rapid heartbeat. A deep sigh or yawn is the body's way of getting more oxygen, whereas shock makes us hold our breath.

When we are deeply relaxed, however, our breathing becomes deeper and slower. In meditation, for example, breathing slows down dramatically and our oxygen intake decreases. Scientists believe that when the breathing quietens, the mind also becomes more tranquil. This idea dates back to the ancient Indian yogis who knew the benefits of controlled breathing and have been reaping the rewards for centuries.

The body thrives on rhythmic, well-spaced breaths that ensure a steady supply of oxygen to the cells. Few of us manage to get through the day without experiencing disruptive emotions, so mastering correct breathing can help to relieve tension and stress. Breathing is one of the simplest and most effective ways of dealing with stress, and yogic breathing, known as *pranayama*, is one of the most effective techniques. Benefitting everyone from high-powered executives to pregnant women or people suffering stress-related illness, breathing is a vital key to unlocking all our deepest anxieties and tensions.

The full yogic breath evokes a deep state of relaxation and allows you to let go of any tension. According to the *Hatha Yoga Pradipika*, an ancient scripture: 'When the breath is irregular, the mind is unsteady, but when the breath is still, so is the mind.'

Most people shallow breathe, which gives rise to feelings of anxiety and confusion and makes it difficult to focus the mind. If we can change to deep breathing, we can think more clearly, deal with people better and avoid dissipating all of our energy. From a physical point of view, correct breathing is energising and rejuvenating as it gives us a sense of well-being.

One of the most effective breath techniques is the full yogic breath, which is ideal for those who need an easy and effective route to deep relaxation. Ideally, it should be practised first thing in the morning and again in the evening if you are feeling tense and tired. It can also be practised during the day before an important meeting, an interview, or whenever you feel unduly stressed.

FULL YOGIC BREATH

1. Lie down in the corpse position with arms placed slightly away from the body, palms turned up, legs relaxed and slightly apart. If you are sitting in a chair, keep the feet flat on floor, shoulders relaxed, waist free.

2. Put your hands lightly on your lower abdomen, taking time to feel the breath expand the stomach.

Let the muscles of the abdomen expand as you inhale and contract as you exhale. Do this for seven breaths.

3. Now rest your hands on your lower ribs, at the sides. Relax your elbows and shoulders to increase the awareness of expansion in the rib cage. Feel your fingers moving upwards and outwards as the rib cage expands. Do this for seven breaths.

4. Place your fingertips on your collar bone and rest them there gently. As you inhale, feel the widening across the collar bone and the expansion across the shoulders.

With practice, this should be done in one complete breath, filling the lower abdomen, the middle chest, then the upper chest with one steady breath, and then exhaling the opposite way. Repeat for at least five full rounds. If you can, relax for a few minutes afterwards to get the full benefits. Incidentally, in yogic breathing, you should inhale through the nose and exhale through the mouth. Try, if possible, to do the exercise on an empty stomach.

The full exercise takes about five minutes, but it will help you to slow down almost instantly and will change your frame of mind. The benefits include correction of shallow breathing, which, in turn, reduces anxiety; maximum lung expansion, which helps to deep-cleanse the body; expansion of lung capacity; and reduction in surface tension, especially in the chest and shoulders. The intake of air is also increased, which stimulates the blood circulation and pumps more oxygen to the brain to improve mental performance. Deep breathing also works on the nervous system and helps to calm and soothe the nerves. Long-term benefits include improved abdominal control and alleviation of digestive problems caused by shallow breathing and abdominal tension.

REVITALISING BREATH

An ancient Indian form of breathing called the *kriyas* is thought to benefit both mind and body. The philosophy behind the *kriyas* is that they are cleansing and energising. In Indian medicine, the breath relates to the body's seven main energy centres, the *chakras,* which are, in turn, linked to the body's major organs.

In western societies, most people breathe from the chest rather than from the diaphragm. This constricts the passage of air through the body, so preventing the free flow of energy.

TAI-JI QI GONG BREATHING EXERCISE

All methods of *qi gong* rely on three main principles:
● adjusting and preparing your posture before you start.
● regulating and controlling the breath.
● calming and quietening the mind.

Before you begin, take a few moments to check your posture. You should stand with feet hip distance apart and parallel, knees slightly bent and arms hanging loosely and relaxed by your sides as if you were suspended by a string of pearls from the ceiling. Then take a few moments to focus on your breath. Inhale deeply through the nose and exhale slowly and steadily through the mouth. Ensure that there are no distractions that will disturb you.

In *qi gong*, the attention is centred on the dantian – a sort of power point located just below the navel. As you breathe in, aim to focus your attention on the dantian.

According to Indian philosophy, ill health is caused by an excess of mucus in the body and stale air in our lungs. Correct breathing helps to cleanse the body and improves the circulation, allowing the body to heal itself and generating much-needed energy. The complete series of *kriyas* is best learned from an experienced teacher. The exercises, however, are quite easy to follow and are an excellent way to get in touch with your breathing.

Qi gong is another eastern breathing technique that is gaining in popularity. A traditional Chinese form of exercise, *qi gong* literally translates as 'breathing exercise'. In China, thousands of people practise it daily, normally first thing in the morning and in their lunch and tea breaks. When practised regularly, *qi gong* helps to clear the mind, aid sleep, enhance mental agility, relieve back pain, regulate breathing, and increase vitality and well-being. *Tai-ji qi gong* is a form of *qi gong* that emphasises a continuous circular breathing pattern, co-ordinated with slow, gentle movement. The movement originates not from muscular force, but from internal energy, the product of breathing and thought. *Tai-ji qi gong* is not just about breathing, it works the muscles and the joints to increase physical fitness. According to *Zhuangzi*, an ancient Taoist work written around 200 BC, 'For the purpose of achieving longevity, breathe deeply with sound, relieve the stale air and take in the fresh. . . .'

SOOTHING BREATH

Natural childbirth guru Frederick Leboyer is an advocate of correct and deep breathing techniques not only during pregnancy and labour but also to help relieve daily stress. Leboyer believes that too much emphasis is put on inhaling deeply, and that exhaling is actually more important because it causes new, oxygen-rich air to enter the body as a reflex action. He also believes that we should breathe from the stomach. Many women consciously hold in their stomachs to keep them flat, and take shallow, insufficient breaths from the chest rather than allowing the breath to inflate the abdomen. He points out that babies and children tend to breathe from their stomachs, making full use of their diaphragms, because they are uninhibited about their body shape. Leboyer encourages deep, abdominal breathing, especially for relieving pain and dispersing tension.

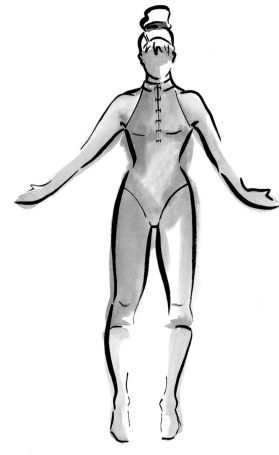

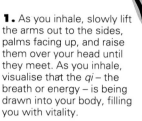

1. As you inhale, slowly lift the arms out to the sides, palms facing up, and raise them over your head until they meet. As you inhale, visualise that the *qi* – the breath or energy – is being drawn into your body, filling you with vitality.

2. Crossing the wrists above your head with palms facing down, exhale very slowly and bring your hands down in front of you, keeping the wrists crossed. Bring them down to the dantian, just below the navel. Keep the movement slow and controlled and focus on the breath filling your body.

LEBOYER'S BREATHING EXERCISE

1. Sit comfortably, either cross-legged on the floor or in a straight-backed chair. Place the palm of the right hand on the stomach, and the left hand against the lower back.

2. As you inhale, allow the breath to push your right hand forwards.

3. Exhale gently and feel the hands moving together, until they feel as if they're almost touching. Rest for a few seconds, then inhale again. Repeat at least 20 times. With practice, this breathing will come automatically.

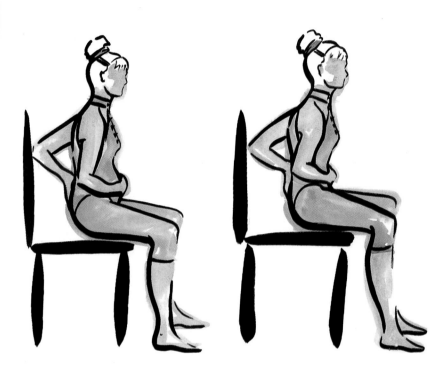

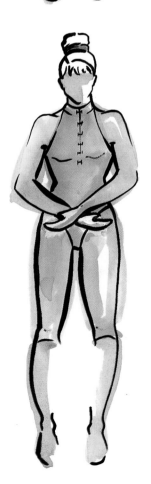

CONSCIOUS BREATHING

1. Sit centred, either on a straight-backed chair or with legs crossed on the floor and with a straight back. Ensure that the spine is straight.

2. Inhale slowly and deeply through the nose, taking the energy down into the body. As you inhale, be aware of the breath passing through the throat and windpipe, into the lungs and diaphragm. Keep your mind on the breath as it travels through the body.

3. Exhale slowly, and consciously follow the breath out of the body. Practise this for at least five full rounds.

YOGA
ACHIEVING PERFECT BALANCE

A balanced combination of relaxation and exercise for both mind and body, yoga is one of the most effective techniques for restoring the body's equilibrium. It is also a technique that has universal appeal and is easily adaptable to suit your own personal needs.

Yoga combines physical, spiritual and mental disciplines and its aim is to achieve perfect balance of mind, body and spirit. This simple and effective technique has been practised in India for thousands of years and has grown in popularity in the West because of the far-reaching benefits associated with regular practice. The word 'yoga' means to unite, and yoga therapy aims – according to ancient Indian philosophy – to unite the five layers, or 'sheaths', of human existence. The first, outer layer represents the physical body; the second layer comprises the vital body – which is made up of *prana*, our life energy; the third layer is the mind and consists of thoughts and emotions; the fourth sheath houses the intellect, which represents perfect thought and knowledge; and the final sheath is believed to be the 'abode of bliss' where we can find inner peace. In yoga therapy, imbalance in any of the sheaths results in disease. However, when you are in a state of optimum health, positive energy is able to flow freely from the 'bliss' sheath to the other layers.

The physical aspects of this spiritual union of mind and body are known as *hatha* yoga. There are a number of different practices under the banner of 'yoga', but *hatha* yoga is the form that most westerners are familiar with. Other forms include *raja* yoga – the yoga of the mind; *mantra* yoga – which uses sound and vibration; and *kundalini* yoga – which aims to releases the body's own 'serpent power', a form of energy that is centred at the base of the spine.

Hatha yoga is a complete system for total health and well-being, combining both physical and psychological aspects. The physical benefits of daily practice are numerous. It helps to build strong muscles, encourages flexible joints and healthy ligaments, and gives greater freedom within the entire torso to allow correct breathing. Physiologically, there is an improvement in all the body's functions, including circulation, digestion and elimination, as well as in the endocrine, reproductive and central nervous systems.

The psychological benefits of yoga are also noticeable and desirable. It encourages a tranquil, calm mind, which facilitates clear thinking, promotes a feeling of inner peace, and helps to control thoughts, feelings and emotions. In a similar way to meditation, it creates a sense of peacefulness that soothes the mind and body, so helping to induce deep, satisfying sleep. Many devotees also notice an ability to focus and concentrate for longer periods of time, without strain.

Yoga is useful in the treatment of many conditions such as arthritis, backache, insomnia, congestion, migraine, indigestion and other debilitating complaints. The following hints will help you to maximise the benefits of regular yoga practice.

● Soak in a warm, scented bath to relax tired muscles and begin to unwind.

● Wear loose, comfortable clothing. Leave the feet bare and remove jewellery, glasses or contact lenses.

● Use a warm, airy room with a clear space. A soft mat or towel makes the warming-up postures more comfortable.

● It is better to practise on an empty stomach. However, you can practise half an hour after a light snack or two to three hours after a meal.

● The best times to practise are in the morning, to remove any stiffness after sleeping and to wake the mind and body; and in the evening, to remove tensions that have built up during the day.

A balanced combination of relaxation and exercise, yoga is one of the most effective techniques for restoring the body's equilibrium, achieving a perfect balance of mind, body and spirit.

WARMING UP

There are three important warm-up exercises, which, together with the following techniques, will enable you to get in touch with your breathing and with the position of your spine. Always breathe slowly and wait for your own individual rhythm to establish itself. It helps to think of the lungs as a pair of balloons, each divided into three sections. Breathe in and the bottom section expands the abdomen; the middle section expands the rib cage and the diaphragm muscle; and the top section expands the upper chest.

Any build-up of tension and anxiety tends to cause shallow breathing, limited to the top part of the chest. For total relaxation, you have to learn to breathe fully and to allow time for the lungs to fill and then empty completely.

When you breathe out, air first leaves the top of the lungs, then the middle, and lastly the bottom. At the very end of the breath, gently squeeze the abdominal muscles in and back towards the spine to empty out the last few puffs of air. After a while, the exhalation will become long and quiet. Then begin the next breath in. The in and out breaths are like two halves of a full circle, which is described as full yogic breathing and has many positive effects. Spend some time familiarising yourself with this deep breathing.

As you lie on the mat practising your breathing (see warm-up positions 1 and 2), begin to picture the spinal column. It is a series of shaped bones or vertebrae, which are smallest in the neck (cervical) region, larger in the middle of the back (thoracic), and largest in the hip (lumbar) area. The spine ends with the tail bone, which curls under the bottom.

The vertebrae alternate with protective discs and are held in place by a network of muscles and ligaments. The spine's degree of flexibility depends on the condition of the supporting muscles and has an overall effect on posture and energy levels.

In warm-up positions 1 and 2, concentrate on the lower spine and, with each breath, allow it to lengthen and flatten against the floor. This particular part of the spine is susceptible to weakness through misuse and it is essential that you spend unhurried time in the warm-up positions.

WARM-UP POSITIONS

1. Lie on mat. Slowly bend knees and place feet hip width apart with heels directly below knees. Relax, soften facial muscles and begin deep breathing. Allow the entire spine to drop to the floor. Pay particular attention to lengthening the lower spine by scooping the front of the hips upwards. (Allow 5 minutes.)

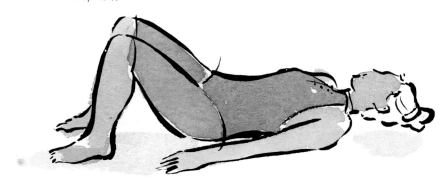

2. Continue to breathe deep, quiet breaths. Drop the left leg down on to mat. Imagine the muscles at the back of this leg being pulled down firmly on to the floor. Slowly bend the right leg and draw the thigh up towards your chest, holding it under the knee. Remember to keep the lower spine in contact with the floor. Then switch legs. (Allow 2–3 minutes on each side.)

3. Begin by standing with your feet hip width apart. Spread the toes of each foot. Move body weight on to heels. At the same time, make the space at the back of the knees very long. As you breathe in and out, feel that your feet are becoming rooted to the floor. Bend forwards from the hips, keeping your weight on your heels with the toes long and wide. Come forwards and down slowly. The hips must stay in line with the heels. Relax the neck, shoulders and arms. As your breathing starts to get deeper, the spine will begin to stretch. Hold the posture for 1 minute, increasing gradually every day until it can be held comfortably for 2 minutes. Breathe in slowly and come up as you breathe.

REBALANCING POSTURES

Yoga expert Lisbeth Russell has devised a rebalancing series of yoga postures, ideal for harmonising both mind and body. 'The primary function of yoga is to balance and focus the mind,' says Russell. 'By concentrating on deep, slow breathing, the mind quietens and becomes calm and clear. This enables awareness to be brought back into the body and rebalances the energy flow, which helps to alleviate tension in the muscles and vital organs. Deep breathing also helps to restore the body's acid and alkaline balance.'

The postures, or *asanas,* have been developed to exercise every muscle, gland and nerve in the body, developing a strong and flexible physique that is geared to maximum health. The rhythm of the *asanas* usually begins with standing and balancing postures and gradually works through to sitting, inverted and, finally, lying down positions.

Each posture should be held for between 45 and 60 seconds and it is vital to take time to get in and out of the positions smoothly and gracefully. Concentrate on breathing at all times – each movement should be done on the exhalation as the breath releases muscle resistance, making it easier to adopt the desired position.

Standing and balancing poses (Tree Pose) establish a sense of external and internal balance and a feeling of inner security, while inverted postures (Spine Release) allow vital organs to receive a fresh supply of blood, help to rest the heart and soothe the nervous system. Inverted poses help to strengthen the spine and lower back, while massaging all the internal organs. Lying poses (Corpse Pose) completely relax and rebalance the mind and body, allowing the release of toxins from the bloodstream.

1. STARTING POSITION (TADASANA)

Stand with feet apart. Spread toes to root feet to the floor. Relax shoulders and let arms drop and hands relax. Fix gaze straight ahead. Breathe deeply and evenly.

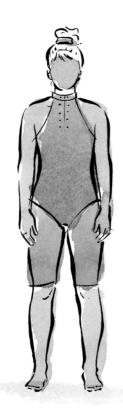

2. TREE POSE (VRKSASANA)

Standing in the starting position, shift weight on to the right foot and secure the sole of the left foot against the right inner thigh. Spread toes, make the standing leg strong, hips facing forwards, and gently pull the knee muscles toward the thigh. Make sure the bent knee is in line with the hip.
Place the hands on the hips, then move the hands to form the prayer position. Lift hands over the head, keeping elbows as straight as possible. Keep chin pointing towards collar bone and keep fingertips and palms together and the backs of the shoulders relaxed.
To help you keep your balance, fix your gaze on a point straight ahead and imagine there is a thread pulling you up.

Benefits: the tree pose helps to improve balance, alignment, concentration and the nervous system. It also strengthens the ankles and firms and tones the leg muscles.

3. TRIANGLE POSE (TRIKONASANA)

Stand with feet apart, turning your toes inwards and keeping toes spread out. The outer edges of the feet should be pressed into the floor. Bring arms to shoulder height and stretch them out. Keeping hips facing forwards, stretch the right arm over the head to the left, placing the other hand on the side of the leg for support. The palm of the hand of the outstretched arm should face the floor. Relax the head and neck.

Benefits: this posture firms and tones the sides and the leg muscles. It trims the waist, expands the chest to facilitate deeper breathing and massages the abdominal organs. It also corrects poor posture.

5. SPINAL RELEASE

Sit on the floor with knees bent. Slowly lower back on to floor vertebra by vertebra, head and back of shoulders relaxing into the floor. Gently pull right knee towards armpit, then left knee, then both knees together. Close the eyes and relax all the muscles in the face.

Benefits: this soothes the mind and helps to stretch the spine gently.

YOGA SEQUENCE

4. SPINE RELEASE (UTTASANA)

Begin in tadasana, place hands on hips, spine straight, backs of shoulders relaxed. Keeping the face up, lower your body towards the floor. Don't try to push all the way. Then take the hands over the head and fold the arms, letting them relax. Relax the shoulders and spine, letting gravity and your breath pull you down. Fix your gaze on the tip of your nose.

Benefits: this helps to stretch and strengthen the spine and releases the hamstring muscles.

6. CHILD'S POSE

Start by sitting on the heels, knees together. Move upper body forwards to rest forehead on the floor. Arms by the sides. Or you can make a pillow with the hands and lightly rest the forehead on hands. Relax all neck and shoulder muscles. Fix gaze at the tip of the nose.

Benefits: a resting pose, this soothes away tension, releases the spine and relaxes the mind and body.

7. CORPSE POSE (SHAVASANA)

Lie on the floor, placing rolled up towel or cushion under knees. This helps the lower back to settle. The whole spine rests down on the floor. Chin points towards the chest, lengthening the back of the neck. Arms by sides, palms facing up. Relax feet and legs and let them drop slightly open. Close your eyes.
Cover yourself with a blanket if you want. Concentrate on breathing deeply and slowly into the stomach, exhaling smoothly and slowly to allow the body to release tension. This pose can be practised on its own for five to 10 minutes when you need to relax and unwind or for three or four minutes at the end of a session.

Benefits: a relaxation pose, this improves breathing, eases the mind and releases tension.

THE SALUTE TO THE SUN

The Salute to the Sun is a sequence of postures that have been combined to create a fluid, harmonised yoga routine. Once you have mastered the basic postures, you can move on to the sequence which combines controlled breathing with steady, stretching movements. Repeat the sequence between six and 12 times, ensuring that you relax between each one – Child's Pose is a suitable relaxation pose. In positions 4 and 9, alternate the feet – i.e. in one round have the right foot forward as in position 4 and the left foot forward as in position 9, as illustrated. In the next round, have the left foot forward in position 4 and right foot forward in position 9. Change over every round. Practise the first four rounds slowly to learn each position precisely. Take your time and don't feel that you have to rush from one position to the next. The middle four rounds can be synchronised with the breath. The last four rounds can be done slightly faster to experience the natural flow of the whole routine. Once you have completed the rounds, relax in Corpse Pose for 10–15 minutes to refresh mind and body.

1. Stand with feet hip width apart. Spread toes and root feet to the floor. Press palms together in the prayer position. Relax shoulders, neck and facial muscles. Check breathing, soften gaze. Begin to exhale as the hands move down and then separate and stretch to each side, as if to brush the sides of a large sun.

2. Inhale. Bring arms above head, thumbs side by side. Feet stay as in position 1.

3. Exhale slowly and come into forward bend (as in warm-up position 3). Keep hips in line with heels and legs straight. Drop head, bringing crown down towards the floor.

4. Inhale. Bend left knee on the floor behind you. Bring right foot directly in between hands, which are shoulder width apart. Spread fingers and press palms firmly against the floor. The bent knee of the right leg must stay in line with the left heel. Drop left hip. Look directly ahead and elongate spine.

5. Hold breath. Bring right foot back to move left. Keep hips above the floor and stretch, keeping legs straight. Lift tail bone towards ceiling and drop heels down to floor, keeping legs straight. Think of the lower spine

lengthening. Drop head and relax neck. Keep arms straight, palms rooted to floor.

6. Exhale slowly. Drop knees, middle of chest bone and forehead to the floor. Only eight points of the body should touch the floor (feet, knees, chest bone, hands and forehead). Think of curling tail bone underneath your bottom and keep lower spine as flat as you possibly can.

7. Inhale. Move body up and between your hands. Relax shoulders and, if more comfortable, bend elbows slightly. Curl tail bone under. Look ahead.

8. Exhale. Repeat second part of position 5, lifting from the tail bone towards the ceiling.

9. Inhale. Repeat position 4, but this time bring the left foot in between hands. Bring right knee on to floor and drop right hip.

10. Exhale. Repeat position 3. Check feet are hip width apart, toes spread and weight falling through heels.

11. Inhale, then repeat position 2 and come up slowly with feet firmly rooted to the floor.

12. Exhale. As if touching the sides of a large sun, bring arms down and hands back as in position 1.

CHAPTER FOUR

MIND, BODY AND SOUL

What is stress and how can we learn to relax? As we enter a new age, the focus is on greater self-awareness. Learning to restore the balance of mind, body and soul can benefit us all and bring us back on to the pathway of optimum health. From meditation to massage, aromatherapy to acupuncture, these age-old treatments all offer potent cures for many common, 20th-century ailments. Learn to relax your mind, de-stress your body and revive your energy levels with soothing therapies that can restore your equilibrium. Or take a look at alternative therapies that seek to treat the root of illness rather than just the symptoms.

STRESS RELIEF
RELAXATION TECHNIQUES TO EASE AWAY TENSION

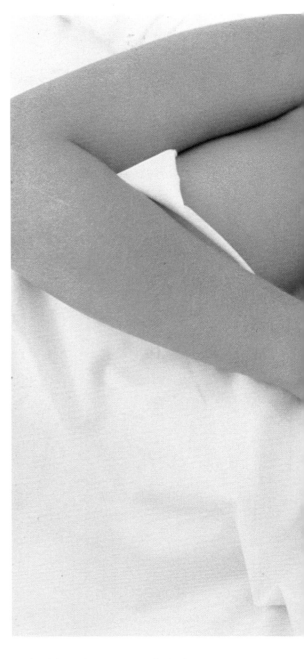

Stress takes its toll on body and soul. But what is stress and what can we do about it? Essentially, stress is really the way in which we react internally to things that are happening externally. In other words, it is our reaction to life. The environment, lack of sleep, insufficient exercise, a poor diet, negative thoughts – these are all elements of stress that are part of our everyday lives.

Some experts have suggested that stress may even have a positive action and that we need an element of stress in order to motivate us and to spur us on. Dr Hans Selye, a leading stress researcher, believes that there are two main levels of stress: 'eustress', which is a moderate, productive kind of stress that gives us energy and encouragement and which he also described as 'the spice of life'; and 'distress', which occurs when we are under too much pressure and start to manifest symptoms of stress-related illness.

But we can learn to control stress by building up our resistance to 'stressors'. We can protect ourselves from physical stressors, such as environmental pollution and extremes in temperature; from chemical stressors, such as additives, pesticides and unsaturated fats; and from biological stressors, such as alcohol, nicotine and caffeine. We can also build up our natural immunity through diet (see Chapter 1, Eating for Vitality). And we can protect ourselves from stress on an emotional and psychological level by learning relaxation techniques, such as massage, yoga and meditation. Relaxation is an essential part of a balanced lifestyle and an excellent means of dealing with stress and maintaining maximum vitality. Energy and vitality come from having a combination of sufficient sleep, nutrients, exercise and relaxation, so it is important that you are able to find enough time each day to spend relaxing.

There are a variety of relaxation methods, from massage to meditation, which can help to alleviate both physical and mental tension. Which method works best for you depends very much on your individual needs. Some find that a good massage does more for them that a session of yoga, while others benefit profoundly from a meditation technique such as transcendental meditation.

The powers of relaxation cannot be underestimated. Those who say they don't need to relax, or that they can't relax, are doing themselves out of a very good thing. Good health depends on balance and, although you may find that you don't need much time to yourself, denying yourself this precious time may eventually have a detrimental effect on your health.

MEDITATION

Meditation aims to cut out the outside distractions of everyday life, allowing the meditator to look within for peace. Regular devotees report improvements not only in their emotional and psychological states, but also in their physical health.

Meditation has been used to achieve a deep sense of tranquillity and, in some cases, altered states of consciousness for thousands of years. There are many forms of meditation, most of which originated in the East – in China, Japan and India. Meditation also exists in other cultures, such as the American Indian and Australian Aborigine, where it is used to achieve a higher state of consciousness and as part of ritual ceremonies.

Good health depends on a balanced lifestyle. That includes a combination of sufficient sleep, exercise, a well balanced diet, and relaxation.

ZEN MEDITATION

The practice of Zen meditation helps to improve self-awareness and relaxes the mind and body. Zen is often used in combination with a daily session of yoga to improve physical fitness.

In Zen meditation, concentration on breathing is the main focus of attention. In Zazen, the practice of meditation, the meditator sits cross-legged on the floor in the Lotus or Half-Lotus position, depending on his or her level of physical fitness. The eyes are left partially open and focus vaguely on a point on the floor about a metre (3 feet) away. You should not concentrate on this external point, but rather focus your attention inwardly.

Next, concentrate on your breathing. Breathe deeply through the nose, ensuring that you fill your diaphragm with air. Breathe calmly and steadily without pausing between inhalation and exhalation. Count each breath or concentrate on it without counting. If you are counting, go from one to 10. Inhale on the odd numbers and exhale on the even numbers. For example inhale – one; exhale – two; inhale – three; and so on. Thoughts and ideas will inevitably spring into your mind during meditation. When you become aware of a thought, take your concentration back to your breathing.

TRANSCENDENTAL MEDITATION

Transcendental meditation was initially brought to the West by Maharishi Mahesh Yogi in the 1960s. In the 1980s in the UK alone, more than 130,000 people were practising TM. The actual process of TM simply involves sitting peacefully for 20 minutes, twice a day, and effortlessly thinking your own *mantra* – a word that has no meaning, but has a life-supporting 'sound' according to ancient Ayurvedic teachings.

Learning TM involves going to an introductory talk, which outlines the theory of meditation along with the benefits. The course itself consists

of four tutorials, spread over four consecutive days, and then a series of regular meditation checks. The first tutorial, when you are given your own *mantra* and taught the mechanics of meditation, is the most important.

Although it is impossible to describe the full process of meditation, the technique involves closing the eyes, being quiet and still and then, after half a minute of silence, beginning to think the *mantra*. While you are meditating, thoughts will still come into your head, but as you become aware of a thought, you simply go back to thinking the *mantra*. Meditators report a sensation of being deeply relaxed as if asleep, yet totally awake and fully alert.

The physiological benefits of TM have been widely documented and go beyond the 20 minutes of meditation. Regular meditators claim that they not only enjoy a greater sense of well-being, improved relaxation and deeper sleep, but that they also experience moments of "total bliss" and are more creatively inspired. Six hundred British doctors have recently recommended that the government makes it available on the NHS, especially for sufferers of stress-related illnesses.

MASSAGE

Touch is one of our most important senses. It creates a bond between mother and child. It makes us feel secure and loved. Massage is the art of touch, a therapy that has deep healing powers for both mind and body. It comforts and reassures, releases muscular tension, boosts the circulation, and makes us feel nurtured and loved. It soothes an overwrought nervous system, while sophisticated methods of stroking, pressing and pummelling unearth buried tensions, melt away aches and pains, flush out toxins, and refine muscle tone. Nothing, it seems, works quite like it for boosting energy and vitality.

The origins of massage lie in the East, namely in China and Japan. Shiatsu, acupressure and reflexology were brought from the East by therapists studying these ancient and highly effective techniques, and have been adopted in the West by alternative practitioners. India also has a strong tradition of massage. Head massage is part of daily life in most Indian regions and is practised even by the most humble barber.

Surprisingly, Swedish massage also originated in the East. Developed by gymnast and physiologist Per Henrik Ling, a Swede who travelled to China in the 19th century, it combined his own western ideas with those of eastern massage.

Eastern philosophies tend to be based on the notion of the flow of energy – the Chinese call it *qi* or *chi* – and massage is the perfect medium for unblocking built-up energy so that the body can be rebalanced and heal itself. Of course, you don't need to go to a therapist for a massage to enjoy the benefits. Self-massage can be just as beneficial, enjoyable and relaxing. You can also use massage to comfort your partner, console a friend, soothe a baby to sleep, or strengthen the bond between you and your child. Massage has far-reaching effects and should become a part of your own relaxation programme.

MASSAGE TECHNIQUES

There are several main strokes involved in massage, although many therapists have developed their own special methods. You can use these basic strokes on yourself and get much of the benefits that you would from a professional masseur, or, of course, when you are massaging someone else.

PETRISSAGE

Pétrissage is a rhythmic rolling, lifting and squeezing of the muscles with the hands. This helps to encourage the flow of nutrients to the area and pumps away built-up toxins and wastes, so easing any pain. Use firm movements and take hold of the flesh between thumb and fingers, pulling it away from the bone and kneading it like a piece of dough. This helps to soothe away tension, especially after strenuous exercise.

TAPOTEMENT

Tapotement or percussion uses slapping, cupping, chopping and hacking hand movements to stimulate or relax the nerves, depending on the length of time for which it is performed. It helps to improve muscle tone and to firm slack skin. It is best used along the backs of the legs and on the back.

EFFLEURAGE

This consists of long, stroking movements, which prepare the skin for touch and are usually used at the beginning and end of a massage session. *Effleurage* warms up the muscles and stimulates both the blood circulation and the lymph flow. Use both hands and slide them gently over the skin while applying an even pressure. The movements are slow and gentle and should help to soothe and comfort.

FRICTION

This movement concentrates on one particular area of tension. Friction consists of rapid strokes with the palms, which help to disperse deep muscular tension. Using firm movements, place the palms on the area to be treated and rub them vigorously back and forth.

Regular meditation promotes a sense of well being, relaxation and deep sleep, allowing you to focus your thoughts and concentrate on achieving your goals.

THE SEQUENCE OF A MASSAGE

BACK MASSAGE

Establish contact by stroking in upward movements, from the buttocks or base of the spine up to the shoulders and neck. Use light, even strokes to begin with, and gradually increase the pressure.

Use friction movements to warm up the muscles and tissues, followed by *pétrissage*. There is little flesh on the back but use the kneading and squeezing movements on the hips, buttocks and shoulders.

Use firm and even finger pressure to stimulate the reflexology points down the neck, shoulder, spine, hips and buttocks. Don't press too hard and check that it is comfortable. Use gentle *tapotement* on the back and more energetic movements on the hips and buttocks.

Finish with long *effleurage* strokes, as if you were stroking a cat, and work your way from the shoulders down the back and buttocks. This has a soothing, calming effect which will often induce sleep.

LEG MASSAGE (BACKS OF LEGS)

Massage each leg individually. Start by stroking lightly down the leg, then up again to the buttocks with a firmer pressure. This will stimulate the blood circulation and lymph flow. Use brisk friction movements on the back of the knee and the ankle. Follow by working on the pressure points on the back of the leg, then use *pétrissage* and *tapotement*.

Stroke down the leg three or four times to the foot and work over the foot with firm, circling movements of the

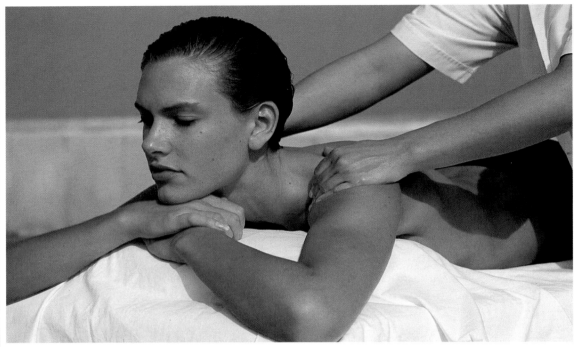

thumbs. Use even pressure on the sole to stimulate the pressure points.

Rub the foot briskly with palms and follow by stroking gently up the leg, buttock, back and shoulder. You should now ask the person to roll over on to their back when they are ready.

ARM MASSAGE

As with the legs, massage one arm at a time.

Start by holding the recipient's hand in your left (or right) hand, and stroke gently from the shoulder to the fingertips. Do this first to the outer arm and then to the inner arm.

Let the arm fall gently down to rest on the bed and use *pétrissage* to work your way up the arm, from wrist to shoulder. Use both hands to knead the flesh and muscle of the upper arm, always working towards the shoulder.

Work your way up the arm, using your thumbs to

stimulate the pressure points. Use firm, even pressure.

Now stroke down the arm and over the hand. Repeat this several times. Massage the hand using the heel of your palm, pressing upwards to the wrist. Use firm, circling movements of the thumbs to press the pressure points on the palms. Massage the fingers, pulling each finger gently towards you with finger and thumb. Stroke the hands gently before you finish.

STOMACH AND CHEST MASSAGE

Start at the neck and stroke downwards, and then outwards across the shoulders. Stroke down the neck, over the collar bone and down the chest, taking care when massaging the delicate tissue of the breasts. Gradually increase the pressure of the strokes and work your way slowly to the midriff.

Use friction over the chest area, circling carefully

around the breasts. Follow by more stroking towards the abdomen. Use the palm of one hand to stroke the abdomen firmly in a clockwise direction. Repeat this about 10 times. Then use *pétrissage* to knead the flesh on the waist and hips. Stroke slowly and firmly from the stomach up the rib cage, gliding the hands down the stomach, and repeat five times. Finish by stroking the whole area, slowly and gently.

THE FRONTS OF THE LEGS

Use the same technique as for the backs of the legs.

HEAD MASSAGE

Head massage can be very relaxing. You can incorporate it into a mini-massage, massaging just the head, shoulders, neck and upper back. Kneel behind the person's head while they are still lying on the floor or sit on a chair

and let them lean their back against your legs. Lightly stroke up the forehead, over the top of the head and down the neck. Repeat this several times. Then work from the temples, across the ears and down either side of the neck. Gradually increase the pressure. Now use your thumbs and fingertips to work up from the forehead to the crown, using small and brisk circular movements. Now use vigorous rubbing movements of the fingertips and work your way over the whole head, down to the neck. Follow by gently stroking the head again, and work your way down the neck and across the shoulders. Allow your hands to rest on the shoulders and press down firmly before you complete the massage. Allow the person to rest for five to ten minutes before they get up. Ask him or her to roll over on to one side and to adopt the fetal position before getting up.

RELEASE AND RELAX

Massage helps to release accumulated tension and works by relaxing tense muscles. Anxiety, stress, emotional upsets and fear all cause muscles to contract and become taut. Most of us experience this tension in the neck, upper and lower back and hips, although individuals may have their own particular tension spots.

Persistent tension causes the muscles to stay

contracted and to become soaked in their own waste products, such as lactic acid. In many cases, this causes pain, impedes function, and prevents freedom of movement.

Athletes can experience similar pain when they are performing, as lactic acid can gather around the hard-working muscles, so causing muscle fatigue. In fact, lactic acid and other wastes are often responsible for the pain and discomfort after any excessive exercise, especially if you push your body beyond its limits. If you exercise sensibly and within your own limitations, the waste products are drained away and don't present a problem.

Massage also helps to ease muscle tension by stimulating blood flow, which in turn helps to carry away any accumulated wastes, and to encourage the delivery of nutrients to and around the muscles. In general, massage improves the circulation. Many of us have sedentary jobs and spend more time sitting and lying down than we do on our feet. This causes sluggish circulation, which can lead to a number of health problems.

When we feel pain, we have a natural reaction to rub, stroke or touch the painful area. Scientists believe that by touching the area, we stimulate receptors in the skin which then send signals to the brain through a gate in the spinal chord. The gate closes before the message reaches it, so alleviating the pain. Another theory is that massage stimulates the release of natural painkillers in the body.

Recent research into the healing powers of touch and massage has revealed that when we touch, or are touched, in a loving way, the brain releases endorphins – chemicals that give us an incredible sense of well-being. It has also been suggested that this kind of healing touch helps to boost the immune system and thus to strengthen the body against illness.

It seems that massage can create a positive and healing attitude, which, combined with love and understanding, can have a powerful effect on our state of health. The distinguished American surgeon, Dr Bernie Siegel, strongly believes in the healing power of touch, especially when it is an expression of love.

He is also convinced, like many doctors, that the mind can heal the body. His work with cancer and AIDS patients has shown remarkable positive results. He has also studied the effects of relaxation techniques on people suffering from illnesses such as asthma, high blood pressure and multiple sclerosis, and has found that the benefits are positive and numerous.

There are no hard and fast rules as to the sequence in which a massage should be performed. Some therapists prefer to start with the feet or back, others with the arms and legs. If you are massaging yourself, you will obviously have to leave out the back, so start with your feet or your neck and shoulders. If you are massaging someone else, ask them where they would prefer you to start – the feet and back are usually the best places to establish initial contact.

AROMATHERAPY

Aromatherapy is not a new treatment. It has been around for over 3,000 years. Based on the use of oils, which are extracted from aromatic herbs, flowers and plants, it works in a number of ways to improve and maintain health. Each plant essence has its own healing properties for the skin and the emotions and they also have powerful cumulative effects on the body's general health.

The history of aromatherapy is shrouded in mystery. Although most people believe that it originated in China, traditional Indian medicine, *ayurveda*, which dates back some 3,000 years, incorporates essential oils into its healing. The Egyptians were also known to use aromatic substances for healing and rituals and it was the temple priests who blended medicines using essential oils for the pharaohs' ailments. The Egyptians also initiated the art of extracting essences from plants by heating them. It was the Greeks, however, who invented distillation, which preserved both the fragrance and the healing properties of the plant for long periods. The Romans continued the tradition of aromatherapy, using oils for massage and to perfume both their homes and spas.

During the Crusades, the knowledge of perfumery and aromatic oils spread, especially in Arabia and the Far East. Arabian chemists perfected distillation and were famous for their exotic fragrances, such as incense, myrrh, sandalwood and musk. One of the most respected pharmacists, Avicenna, was the first to distil essence of rose, which is still the most expensive oil as it takes up to 1,000 kg (500 lb) of rose petals to make 500 g (1 lb) of essence. The crusaders brought back many of the methods and techniques of aromatherapy to Europe. During the Great Plague, the essences of pine, cypress and cedar were burned in hospitals, sickrooms and even in the streets to ward off the virus.

The plundering of South America brought even more knowledge of essential oils. The Aztecs were famous for their medicinal concoctions and the Spanish discovered a wealth of knowledge about herbalism from Montezuma's botanical gardens. The North American Indians had also devel-

THE PROPERTIES OF ESSENTIAL OILS

BASIL
Basil is a powerful anti-depressant. It is also an excellent antiseptic, a tonic for the digestion, and helps to stimulate the adrenal glands which control hormone production. Use it to treat fatigue, nausea, migraine, depression and tension.

BAY
A potent decongestant, tonic and antiseptic, bay is ideal for treating colds and 'flu, and for easing congested lung conditions. It is also an age-old remedy for scalp disorders.

BERGAMOT
Antiseptic, astringent and anti-depressant qualities. Excellent for rebalancing oily skins and for calming acned skin. Avoid using prior to sunbathing as it sensitises the skin to UV light. Use to stimulate, uplift, and revive flagging spirits.

BORAGE OIL
The richest source of gamma linolenic acid and essential fatty acids. Used to treat skin discorders such as eczema and psoriasis.

CHAMOMILE
Soothes and calms the nerves. Relieves pain and aids digestion. Chamomile contains azulene, which has anti-bacterial and healing properties. Use it to soothe inflamed skin, to relieve nervous tension, neuralgia and digestive disorders, and as a relaxant to promote sleep.

CEDARWOOD
Used for centuries as an antiseptic, sedative, digestive stimulant and aphrodisiac. Treats eczema, dry skin, and lung congestion. Stimulates sexual responses.

EUCALYPTUS
This oil has antiseptic properties, is a natural stimulant, repels insects, and soothes mucous membranes.
It helps to alleviate 'flu, sinus, throat and chest problems and can be used as a disinfectant in the home.

FRANKINCENSE
A very ancient essence, it calms, induces relaxation and sleep, and alleviates respiratory conditions.
Use to treat insomnia, dry skin and nervous tension.

GERANIUM
Diuretic, astringent and anti-depressant, geranium stimulates the adrenal glands and relieves pain.
Ideal for treating poor circulation, healing burns and wounds and soothing inflamed tissue. It is also an excellent skin tonic.

JASMINE
Aphrodisiac, anti-depressant and soothing. Use in labour to stimulate contractions, and after birth to discourage post-natal depression. Excellent skin soother.

JUNIPER
Diuretic and antiseptic, juniper also stimulates the digestion and tones the nervous system.
Use to treat fatigue, sluggish digestion, water retention and rheumatism.

LAVENDER
Analgesic and calming to the cerebrospinal area. Calming and soothing. Antiseptic and antibacterial. Use to treat nervous conditions, headaches, and general aches and pains. Also soothes acne and insect bites.

MYRRH
Healing, antiseptic, astringent and a tonic for the nervous system. Myrrh helps to heal wounds, eases coughs, soothes mouth and skin ulcers, and combats general infections.

NEROLI
A natural sedative, neroli is also an anti-depressant and an aphrodisiac.
Alleviates depression, insomnia, nervous tension and digestive upsets. Soothing for dry skin.

PATCHOULI
Has antiseptic, anti-depressant and sedative properties. Patchouli also relieves anxiety, soothes minor skin conditions and peps up the circulation.

PEPPERMINT
Stimulates the nervous system, aids digestion, and acts as an anti-spasmodic. Relieves indigestion and flatulence, soothes headaches, and alleviates fatigue. Also good for asthma and bronchitis.

PETITGRAIN
Calming, sedative and refreshing. Helps to treat anxiety, stress, tension and insomnia.

PINE
Diuretic, antiseptic, and stimulates the adrenal glands. Treats minor infections, water retention, and depression. Excellent for cleansing and disinfecting the home environment.

oped their own herbal remedies and used essential oils in cleansing ceremonies.

In the 19th century, scientists began to research the effects of essential oils on bacteria. It was a French chemist, René Maurice Gattefosse, who started serious research into the use of essential oils to heal, and he coined the word aromatherapy in 1928.

Another Frenchman responsible for the development of aromatherapy was Doctor Jean Valnet, a medical doctor who discovered Gattefosse's research and began experimenting with various oils with his patients. At around the same time, a French biochemist, Marguerite Maury, developed methods of applying the oils to the skin with massage. Micheline Arcier, now resident in London, studied with Maury and Valnet and combined their techniques to create a modern aromatherapy technique that is now used by therapists all over the world.

Aromatherapy can be used to heal in three main ways: through massage, through inhalation, and through oral administration in herbal infusions or in cooking. It is best not to take essential oils orally unless you are under the supervision of a highly skilled therapist or doctor. Essential oils are potent and could be harmful if used without proper knowledge.

MASSAGE

Massage is the most powerful medium for aromatherapy. In aromatherapy massage, essential oils are applied to the skin and worked into the skin using techniques that centre around the nervous system and the channels of energy or meridians, which were discovered centuries ago by the Chinese. The massage aims to unblock trapped energy by releasing muscle tension, thus letting the energy flow freely around the body and stimulating the body's main organs, glands, nerves, and blood and lymphatic circulation. Depending on which essential oil is used, the result can be either invigorating or soothing.

The oils are not only beneficial to the skin – soothing, healing, stimulating and moisturising it. They also have a deep-reaching effect because they

ROSE
Antibacterial, regulates female hormones, anti-depressant, and astringent.
Good for all skin types. Stimulates libido, relieves headaches and insomnia, and alleviates nausea.

ROSEMARY
Decongestant, stimulant, promotes clear thinking and encourages memory function. Use to treat colds, 'flu and chest infections. Also soothes headaches and rheumatism, sores and burns.

SAGE
Regulates female hormone balance, diuretic, tonic, antiseptic, thought to control blood pressure. Treats nervous tension, low blood pressure, bronchitis, and menopausal disorders.

SANDALWOOD
Aphrodisiac, tonic and antiseptic. Excellent for treating fatigue, digestive upsets, and skin problems such as acne.

SWEET MARJORAM
The mild light aroma of this oil is widely used for its healing properties and to help people to overcome grief. Its warming properties are soothing, calming and act as a sedative.

TANGERINE
Energising, anti-depressant, tonic. Excellent during pregnancy. Also one of the best oils for children. Relieves depression, fatigue and tension.

TEA TREE
This oil has powerful antiseptic, fungicidal and skin-healing properties. Treats scalp conditions, cuts, burns, minor infections, acne and boils.

VETIVER
One of the most soothing oils, it calms and relaxes. Relieves tension, sleeplessness and anxiety.

YLANG YLANG
Anti-depressant, sedative, regulates blood pressure. Good for nervous tension and hypertension, stimulates libido and uplifts spirits.

PLANT OIL PROPERTIES

The carrier plant oils are vegetable oil bases in which essential oils are dissolved.

ALOE VERA
Has the same pH as skin and is well known for its healing properties.

APRICOT KERNEL
Rich in mineral salts and vitamin A, it helps to keep skin smooth.

AVOCADO
Rich in vitamins A and B, it is a suitable moisturiser for sensitive skins.

EVENING PRIMROSE
Rich in vitamins E and F, it improves skin texture and helps to heal blemishes.

HAZELNUT
Has a high level of mineral salts which help to soothe the skin.

JOJOBA
Contains a high level of waxy substances, which mimic the skin's own collagen and help to keep it supple.

PEACH KERNEL
A rich moisturiser for sun-parched and mature skins.

SESAME SEED
Helps to absorb the sun's harmful UV rays and has soothing and moisturising properties.

SWEET ALMOND
An emollient oil which benefits nails, hair and skin.

VITAMIN E
A healing oil reputed to have anti-ageing properties. Use it liberally on face and body.

WHEATGERM
Contains vitamins A, B, C and E, which help to alleviate blemishes and to firm and tone skin tissue.

AROMATHERAPY BLENDS

RELAXING BATH
4 drops of lavender, 4 drops of patchouli and 2 drops of rose.

SENSUAL BATH
4 drops of jasmine, 4 drops of ylang ylang and 2 drops of sandalwood.

CLEANSING BATH
Add 2 drops of eucalyptus, 2 drops of pine and 2 drops of geranium to a hot bath to relieve colds and 'flu.

SOOTHING BATH
Soothe aches and pains with 4 drops of chamomile, 2 drops of lavender and 4 drops of geranium.

UPLIFTING BATH
4 drops of neroli, 2 drops of rose and 2 drops of sandalwood.

PREGNANCY BATH
Combine 6 drops of tangerine, 2 drops of geranium and 2 drops of neroli to uplift the spirits and soothe the skin.

OILS FOR THE SKIN

DRY SKIN
Blend 13 ml (½ fl oz) of wheatgerm oil with 13 ml (½ fl oz) of avocado oil and 50 ml (2 fl oz) of a bland vegetable oil, such as sesame or almond oil. Add four drops of lavender and four drops of rose or geranium to four drops of sandalwood. Add the oil from a vitamin E capsule for an extra moisturising treat.

OILY SKIN
Add four drops of sage, 4 drops of chamomile and four drops of basil to 75 ml (3 fl oz) of safflower or sunflower oil.

COMBINATION SKIN
Add four drops of ylang ylang, two drops of geranium and 2 drops of neroli to 50 ml (2 fl oz) of jojoba oil.

stimulate the olfactory receptors located in the nose. These receptors send messages to the brain's limbic system, which is the master controller of many other brain functions, such as the heart rate, breathing, blood pressure, sexual organs, memory and stress response. The oils can actually affect how we feel, what we think and how we deal with stress.

Scientists are researching the effects of essential oils on the limbic system and are studying their effects on patients suffering from severe depression and other disorders of the nervous system. Aromatherapy is also being encouraged in hospitals to soothe patients with heart conditions, to calm hyperactive children, and to stimulate those with severe depression or suffering from physical symptoms of withdrawal.

INHALATION
The oils can also be used by themselves, without massage, to stimulate the olfactory receptors. They can be added to hot water in the bath, to soothe or to stimulate, or they can be inhaled in a basin of

steaming water to clear the sinuses and soothe congested chests. They can also be used to steam-cleanse your face in a facial sauna, so helping to calm, moisturise and regulate both skin texture and tone.

These are just a selection of the best-known and most widely-available essential oils. You will probably come across other variants, depending on your suppliers. It is difficult to find high-quality oils and, when you do, they are usually very expensive. Keep your oils in a cool, dark place. They should come in dark, glass bottles to protect them from the light. Never leave them where they are exposed to heat or light, as this will destroy their healing properties.

It is also important to remember that most oils will already be diluted in a base or carrier oil. This will be a bland oil, such as almond, safflower or wheatgerm oil. Check whether your essential oil is pure or has been diluted before applying it directly to your skin. You should always dilute the essences with a carrier oil before application to the skin to avoid an allergic reaction.

You can blend two or three oils together, depending on the result you want. Experiment to find the most relaxing combination or the most reviving blend. Two or three drops of each oil are all you will need. Use the chart as a guide to find out which oils are best to alleviate your particular problem, be it physical or psychological. Use the oils for massage, bathing or inhalation.

CARRIER OILS

Carrier oils are vegetable in origin, derived from plants, nuts and vegetables. Plant oils are an excellent way in themselves to treat skin and their versatility allows them to be used on both skin and hair. Not to be confused with essential oils, plant oils include aloe vera, apricot kernel, avocado, evening primrose, jojoba, sesame seed and sweet almond oil. Essential oils are also derived from plants but are aromatic, volatile essences. Always combine essential oils with a carrier oil before you apply them to the skin.

THE BEAUTY OF OILS

Many vegetable oils are so fluid that they are absorbed into the skin in minutes. They help to reinforce the skin's own lipid layer, which helps to prevent moisture loss. Oils rich in certain nutrients are particularly beneficial. Linoleic acid, a constituent of vitamin F, is obtained from olive, sunflower, sesame, hazelnut and almond oil. Linoleic acid strengthens the membrane surrounding skin cells once it has been converted into GLA – gamma linoleic acid – by the skin's enzymes. GLA is also an important nutrient, essential to the healthy functioning of the body.

An excellent tip for cleansing dry, fragile skin is to smooth on a little jojoba or sesame oil, massage it into the skin and wash it off with a non-detergent cleansing bar and plenty of warm water. This emulsifies any residue on the skin without dehydrating it. Even those with oily skin should not shy away from oils. In many cases, they have been found to balance the production of sebum in the skin and can therefore have a calming effect for acne sufferers.

Massage the oils into skin which has been thoroughly cleansed. After steaming is an ideal time, when skin is warm and receptive to the oils. Use gentle upward and outward strokes, starting from the throat and working up from the chin to the forehead. Then use small circular movements which will help absorption. Finish off by tapping your fingertips lightly over the whole face to stimulate the circulation.

The therapist uses her fingertips to apply gentle pressure to the temples to relax facial muscles and soothe deep-seated tension.

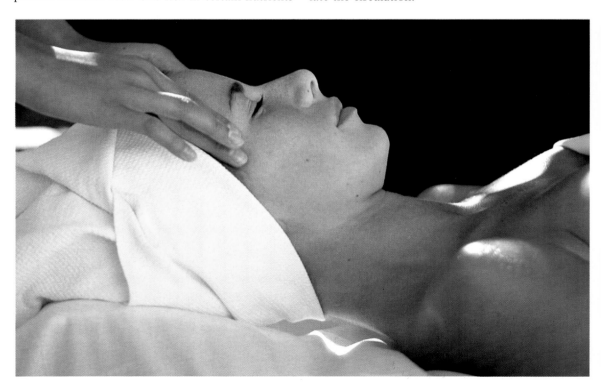

ALTERNATIVE TREATS
THERAPIES DESIGNED TO REBALANCE MIND & BODY

More and more people are looking towards alternative or complementary medicine for a solution to their health problems. At the root of most alternative therapies lies the basic philosophy that, in order to achieve perfect health, one must sustain a balance between mind, body and spirit. Most alternative therapies originated in the East, but there are also a number of therapies with western origins. They all share a common resolution – that prevention is far more desirable than cure. Although there are numerous treatments, the following outlines a few of the most common and the most widely available therapies.

REFLEXOLOGY

Reflexology dates back thousands of years, when it was used by ancient Chinese practitioners to treat and diagnose illnesses. References were also made to this method of healing, using pressure points located on the hands and feet, in ancient Egyptian records – there are detailed drawings demonstrating its use in the Tomb of the Physician, which date back to 2300 BC.

Modern reflexology has its roots in the early 20th century, when Dr William Fitzgerald, an eminent American physician, studied the relationships between the body and the hands and feet. His findings suggested that there were specific interactions between zones on the hands and feet and the major organs of the body and that, by pressing these areas, he could directly affect the relevant organs. Further research determined that the interactions followed a logical pattern.

In reflexology or zone therapy, the body is divided into zones or energy channels, five on either side of the body's midline, which run vertically through the body and end in the feet. Any part of the body can be stimulated by working on the reflex area of the feet in the same zone. For example, by pressing the inner edges of the feet, it is possible to stimulate the spine, which is in the same zone. This means that the hands and feet can be used to communicate with the rest of the body.

According to the theory, a poor diet, a sedentary lifestyle or illness causes congestion in the feet, resulting in the deposit of small crystalline-like lumps around the nerve endings. By using deep pressure with the fingers, therapists can break down these lumps, which are believed to be made up of accumulated waste materials. The deposits

can then be eliminated from the body through the bloodstream, so boosting the circulation and promoting blood supply to the rest of the body. Reflexologists also believe their technique can be used as a diagnostic tool. The therapist can use tender areas in the feet to pinpoint crystalline deposits and so to discover the cause of a health problem and which part of the body it stems from. For health maintenance, reflexologists recommend that a daily foot massage can help to keep the body healthy and act as a tonic. It also promotes relaxation and relieves tension and stress.

Today, more than 6,000 European doctors, nurses and physiotherapists combine reflexology with their own healing techniques. It can help to relieve pain, to encourage effective relaxation and to encourage the body to heal itself more efficiently. It has still not been discovered exactly how or why reflexology works, but therapists who practise reflexology believe that it helps to re-establish the body's equilibrium by maintaining correct metabolic balance.

REFLEX OR PRESSURE POINTS

Apart from Fitzgerald's work on zone therapy, Eunice Ingham was also important in developing modern reflexology. A physiotherapist/masseuse in the 1930s, Ingham mapped out areas on the feet that corresponded to the rest of the body. The areas or reflex points can then be stimulated by

Reflexology pressure points on the hands and feet are used to discover the root of an illness. The points can be stimulated to treat as well as to diagnose.

D.I.Y. REFLEXOLOGY WORKOUTS

When practising reflexology on your own feet, use your middle finger or your thumb to exert a firm, even pressure on each reflexology point. You may feel a little discomfort, but this is nothing to worry about.

FATIGUE
Press on each foot

Brain	10 times
Liver	10 times
Adrenal Gland	10 times
Lung	10 times
Heart Reflex	10 times

on the left foot only.

HEADACHES

Brain	10 times
Pancreas	10 times
Spine	10 times
Solar plexus	10 times

CONSTIPATION

Solar plexus	10 times
Stomach	15 times
Pancreas	15 times
Liver	15 times
Adrenal gland	10 times
Intestines	15 times

MENSTRUAL CRAMPS

Solar plexus	10 times
Thyroid gland	10 times
Spine	10 times
Uterus	10 times

PREMENSTRUAL TENSION

Pituitary Gland	10 times
Brain	10 times
Thyroid	10 times
Adrenal gland	10 times
Kidneys	10 times
Ovaries	15 times
Uterus	15 times

STRESS

Solar plexus	15 times
Pituitary Gland	15 times
Thyroid gland	15 times
Lungs	15 times
Kidneys	15 times
Spine	10 times

COLDS AND FLU

Pituitary Gland	15 times
Sinuses	15 times
Ears	15 times
Lungs	10 times
Adrenal glands	10 times
Lymphatic system	15 times

INSOMNIA

Solar plexus	15 times
Brain	15 times
Thyroid Gland	15 times
Spine	15 times

NAUSEA

Solar plexus	10 times
Brain	15 times
Ears	15 times
Stomach	15 times
Intestines	15 times

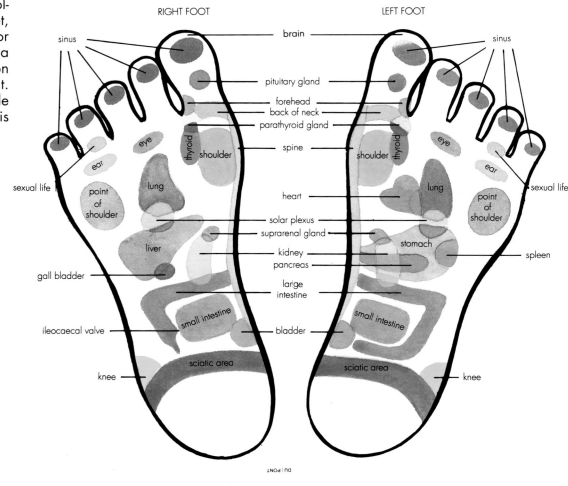

RIGHT FOOT — LEFT FOOT

sinus · brain · sinus · pituitary gland · forehead · back of neck · parathyroid gland · spine · eye · thyroid · shoulder · shoulder · thyroid · eye · ear · ear · sexual life · point of shoulder · lung · heart · lung · point of shoulder · sexual life · solar plexus · suprarenal gland · liver · kidney · pancreas · stomach · spleen · gall bladder · large intestine · small intestine · small intestine · ileocaecal valve · bladder · sciatic area · sciatic area · knee · knee

DU PONT

finger pressure to treat and diagnose a variety of health problems.

Although it is obviously preferable to see a trained reflexologist, you can benefit greatly from zone therapy by stimulating the reflex points on your hands and feet yourself. Apart from anything else, hand and foot massage can be very relaxing and can help to alleviate minor health problems.

Each reflex point on the foot will stimulate the major organ in the same zone. Some organs have corresponding reflex points on only one foot. Ensure that you are pressing the correct points by referring to the chart.

Use the side of the tip of your thumb to press the required reflex point. Each point is clearly marked on the reflexology map. Use firm, even pressure, moving your thumb in small, circular movements, or repeatedly pressing and then releasing to stimulate the reflex. You don't need to use oil on the feet, but you can dust them with a little talcum powder.

ACUPUNCTURE

Acupuncture is part of the traditional medicine of China. It is based on a philosophy very different from that of western medicine and, over the last 3,000 years, its practitioners have developed a unique understanding of how the whole body works. The aim of acupuncture is to correct the flow of *qi* or *chi* – the body's vital energy. This keeps the blood circulating, warms the body, fights disease, and links all parts and functions together so that they can work in harmony. There are 12 main *chi* meridians, or channels, each connected to an internal organ and named after that organ. They follow a set pathway in the body. When a person is healthy, the *chi* moves smoothly through the channels. If, for some reason, the flow is blocked, or is too weak or too strong, then illness occurs.

In determining a pattern of disharmony, the acupuncturist needs a detailed picture of the patient's lifestyle, diet, work, medical history and emotional state. The diagnosis includes questioning, observation and examination of the pulses and the tongue. Pulse and tongue diagnosis are highly refined in Chinese medicine.

The pulses are felt on the insides of the wrists and there is one for each of the 12 energy channels. The strength, rhythm and quality of a pulse indicates the balance or imbalance of energy and state of health or disease. The tongue, through its shape, colour, movement and coating, is used to indicate the progression and degree of an illness.

When the acupuncturist has established a diagnosis, he can then start to rebalance the *chi* by inserting fine needles into particular points on the channels. This effects a change in a part or function of the body, which stimulates the body's natural healing powers. The practitioners may also use moxibustion – burning herbs on the skin, on or around key points – to stimulate energy. This is used as a supplement to the needles.

Acupuncture is effective in treating a variety of chronic, painful and infectious disorders, from bronchitis, hepatitis and tetanus to allergies, arthritis, irregular menstrual periods, migraine, depression, kidney stones, hormonal and nervous disorders. Acupuncture is preventative as well as curative, as practitioners are trained to recognise disease long before the patient becomes aware of any illness. It can also be used to treat children, and pregnant women can be treated for complications in pregnancy without causing harm to mother or baby. It can also be effectively combined with western medicine.

OSTEOPATHY

Osteopathy is a manipulation therapy, which works on the alignment of the joints, muscles and ligaments. It is based on a theory that maintains that many health problems are triggered by mechanical faults in the basic structure of the body. When joints are frozen and muscles are lacking in tone or are in spasm, they can interfere with the functioning of the nerves, the blood supply and the drainage systems of bodily organs.

During an initial consultation, the practitioner will carefully study the alignment of the body. He will look for tight contractions in the muscles, twists and breaks in the fluid nature of the spine, and bones and joints that appear to be misshapen or out of natural symmetry.

Treatment to restore natural movement and posture to the joints consists of a series of manipulation and leverage techniques, which free tensions, relax spasms and return bones and joints to their natural positions. Osteopathy is effective in treating badly contracted muscles and ligaments, structural damage due to accidents, spinal injuries and trapped nerves, and in correcting pelvic alignment, especially during pregnancy.

CRANIAL OSTEOPATHY

Cranial osteopathy is a gentle therapy that aims to release inner cranial tensions and correct imbalances in neuro-muscular functioning. Serious cranial damage can occur through car accidents, from childhood and sports injuries, and even from the appliance of forceps during birth. This type of structural damage can be the cause of many problems resulting from cranial tension and the restriction of the cerebrospinal fluid which bathes the brain and the spinal cord.

A cranial osteopath will apply a series of subtle movements that work to soothe away trapped energy and compounded stress in order to allow the head, facial and neck bones and muscles to return to their natural state and order. As a result, brain impulses and nerve functions can flow freely, together with an improved circulation of the blood and cerebrospinal fluid. After a series of treatments, it is often possible to see a difference in the shape of a face that has been damaged due to accidental injury. Cranial osteopathy is effective in relieving headaches, migraine, poor co-ordination, nervous disorders and stiff muscles.

SHEN TAO

Shen tao is an ancient form of acupressure based on traditional Oriental medicine. It is similar to acupuncture, although it is not invasive. Instead of using fine needles to rebalance energy, the fingers and hands are used to redirect the *chi* via specific pressure points along the network of energy channels, or meridians, that run throughout the body. *Shen tao* is often so subtle that one can hardly believe the therapist is actually doing anything. Usually only two points at a time are pressed, often in different locations on the body but connected by the same meridian. It is, however, very powerful and changes in energy can often be felt during a session. People often comment on feelings of weightlessness, as if they are floating, and of a sense of peace and tranquillity, while others experience a rush of energy, similar to that of adrenalin. Sometimes a rapid revitalisation and relief from a complaint is experienced, while for others healing may take a slow, steady course to restore well-being.

Initially there is a detailed consultation, which explores the background to a patient's current condition. This includes documentation of medical history, diet, lifestyle and emotional state. The practitioner will use Chinese pulse diagnosis to complete the overall picture. *Shen tao* attempts to harmonise mind, body and spirit by treating deep-seated imbalances occurring within the physical and emotional bodies. It works to relieve current symptoms at their original source.

The therapy is deeply relaxing and works to trigger the body's natural healing capacity. It helps to soothe, and releases many forms of stress, both emotional and psychological. It is an effective treatment for many stress-related illnesses, such as migraine, menstrual disorders, high blood pressure, and muscular tension.

SHIATSU

Shiatsu massage originated in China approximately 3,000 years B.C. and was later developed in Japan. Unlike traditional massage, which works by soothing and relaxing muscles, *shiatsu* works to harmonise and balance the *chi,* or energy, which travels through the body's 12 meridians. It is practised as a healing art and stimulates the body's capacity to heal itself. The aim of *shiatsu* is to remove any energy blockages or tension within the body, which might interrupt the free flow of *chi*. In a similar way to reflexology, the fingers and hands, elbows, knees and feet are all employed to stimulate the energy channels at pressure points, or *tsubos*. An experienced *shiatsu* practitioner starts by looking at areas where the body is physically unbalanced and where the *chi* is not flowing smoothly. This is evident from the shape and formation of the body, and it is also possible to examine the face to determine tensions held within the body. The practitioner then uses a variety of techniques, varying from subtle and supportive contact to more dynamic pressure, including stretching, kneading, rubbing and pressing of the pressure points to relax the body and help the energy to flow unhindered.

After *shiatsu* massage, the body may feel cold. Massage takes energy from where there is a surplus and redirects it to areas where it is depleted. As a result, muscles, joints and blood flow are positively influenced, thus increasing circulation, flexibility and overall vitality. *Shiatsu* releases physical and emotional tensions, leaving the mind and body balanced and relaxed. It is helpful for any stress-related illness and for physical tension, PMT, asthma, digestive disorders and poor circulation.

FLOTATION

Although flotation was first used as a therapy in the 1950s, it is fast becoming one of the most popular alternative therapies. Devised by American doctor John Lilly, flotation, or sensory deprivation, consists of floating on your back in 25–30 cm (10–12 inches) of salty, buoyant water in a small, dark enclosed chamber. This may sound like a nightmare to many people, but those who have experienced flotation believe it to have a deeply relaxing effect on mind, body and spirit. New Age music is often played as you float and, at some flotation centres, coloured lights may be used to soothe and calm the mind

There are several explanations to suggest why floating works as a natural relaxant. Some researchers believe that floating triggers the brain's production of endorphins, natural painkillers that are produced mainly by the pituitary gland and which promote feelings of deep relaxation, contentment and euphoria. Endorphins are also produced during acupuncture, shiatsu, massage and meditation and even during lovemaking, vigorous exercise and childbirth.

It is thought that removing the force of gravity stimulates natural chemical changes, although this has not yet been proved. Experiments have shown that immersion in water reduces levels of adrenalin and other chemicals that are produced when we are cold or frightened, and that water has a positive, comforting effect that may remind us of our time in the womb.

Flotation is excellent for those who enjoy water and don't mind being in small, enclosed spaces but is not advisable for those with phobias about either. Because of its relaxing action, it is beneficial in alleviating tension, insomnia, anxiety and other psychological disturbances.

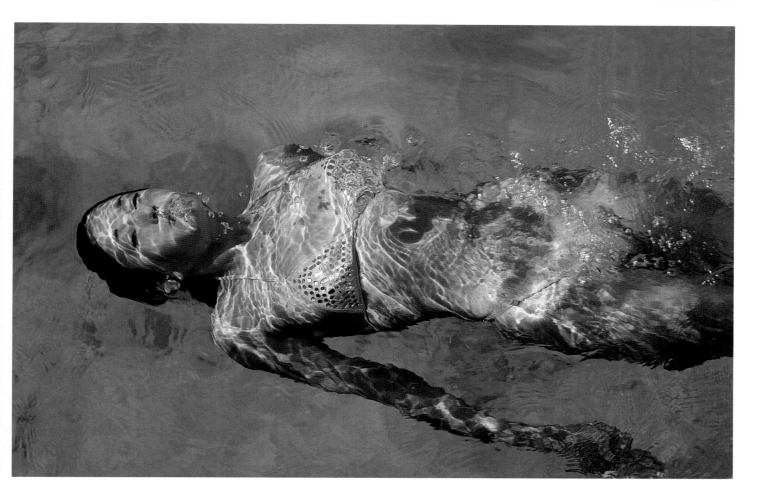

CHIROPRACTIC THERAPY

Chiropractics is used to treat a variety of muscle and joint-related disorders by using manipulation or by adjusting the spine and joints. The aim of a chiropractor is to treat the root of a problem and not just the symptoms. An initial diagnosis is made by recording the patient's medical history and then conducting a physical examination. The spine is palpated to detect areas of immobility and x-rays may be taken.

Once a diagnosis has been made, the therapist works to restore the correct biomechanical position and movement of the spine by releasing any muscular tension or strain using quick and precise movements. The movements aim to release pressure on trapped spinal nerves, which is the most common cause of discomfort.

Several treatments may be necessary in order to alleviate the cause of pain and patients often find that their digestive and respiratory systems improve, as well as their menstrual cycles. Chiropractics is used to treat back and neck pain, headaches and migraine, frozen shoulders, arthritis, knee, ankle and other joint pain.

HOMEOPATHY

Orthodox or allopathic medicine is usually geared to treating symptoms rather than the root cause of an illness, whereas holistic therapies, such as homeopathy, seek to discover the origin of the illness. Homeopathy takes a holistic approach to disease and examines the patient as a whole — lifestyle, diet, exercise and emotional state are all taken into account.

Homeopathy means 'like disease', whereas allopathy, or orthodox medicine, means 'opposite disease'. In homeopathy, medicines actually produce the symptoms of the disease that the homeopathic doctor is trying to treat, and the underlying philosophy is 'like cures like'.

Developed in the 19th century by a German doctor called Samuel Hahnemann, homeopathy established that symptoms are outward manifestations that the body is fighting illness from within. He aimed to create a medicine that would firstly enhance the symptoms of a disease, and then secondly cure it.

To prove his theory, he tested various substances derived from natural sources on himself, and on his friends and family. To determine what substance could cure what, he had to create the symptoms of an illness in a healthy person by using homeopathic medicine.

The treatment that he devised takes the form of dilute amounts of the chosen remedy. The substances are thought to work more potently than other drugs because of the complex process of dilution involved in making homeopathic medicines. Homeopaths believe that the more dilute the preparation, the more powerful its healing properties. Homeopathy is used to treat as wide a range of ailments as orthodox medicine.

Flotation allows the body to be free from gravity, so encouraging the muscles to relax and in turn releasing tension.

CHAPTER FIVE

TOTAL SKIN CARE

Let's face it: only nature can create a perfect, flawless complexion. But a well-balanced diet, sufficient sleep, regular exercise and a meticulous skin care regime can all contribute to making the most of your natural assets and creating a healthy, clear complexion. So take positive action. If you want beautiful skin, it is essential that you follow a skin care routine, coupled with a balanced diet and regular exercise. The importance of deep cleansing, both internally and externally, can never be over-emphasised – especially if you live in a city, where your skin is open to attack from harmful environmental elements. and even perfect skin needs to be protected and preserved to maintain a healthy bloom.

Skin is a living organ, which reflects your inner health. If you abuse your body, your complexion is always the first to suffer. Overloading with pollutants such as alcohol, coffee, tea, the chemicals involved in the processing of food, medical drugs and cigarette smoke, together with a poor input of essential nutrients, leaves the skin looking dull, lifeless and all too often covered with blemishes. Add to this an overdose of stress or lack of fresh air, exercise, sunshine and sleep, and you could end up with the sort of skin problems that no cosmetic preparation can ever hope to solve.

Efficiently functioning kidneys, intestines and liver are vital to skin texture and clarity. The liver not only manufactures the substances that help remove waste products from the body, but also detoxifies it of certain drugs, chemicals found in food, drink and water, and poisons produced by bacteria and viruses. When overworked and burdened with fatty foods, alcohol or emotional upsets such as worry, nervousness, anger and frustration, the liver's efficiency is reduced. As a result, toxins can accumulate in the blood and can be dumped in the skin for elimination, causing it to look blotchy and blemished.

A two-day fruit, vegetable and water fast will help to give the liver a rest and activate the other organs of elimination. Citrus fruits such as lemons, oranges, grapefruit and limes are particularly useful. They help fortify the liver and are also rich in vitamin C, one of nature's most potent detoxifiers. Young dandelion leaves offer an excellent treatment for liver congestion and are powerful blood cleansers, as are watercress and parsley, with their high vitamin C and trace mineral content, and most green leafy vegetables.

Encourage the kidneys to flush away toxins by drinking plenty of pure spring water – forget tap water as it contains numerous chemicals. The kidneys also need a good supply of the mineral potassium to work well. Good food sources include potatoes, spinach, bananas, raisins, asparagus and peaches.

The swift passage of food through the intestine is vital to the cleansing process, as when food lingers too long, wastes start to be absorbed back into the bloodstream. Roughage, which is present in the leaves, stalks and roots of vegetables as well as in the skins and seeds of fruits, speeds up this movement considerably.

Try to shop for organically grown varieties of fruit and vegetables, which have not been sprayed with chemicals. These tend to be concentrated in the fruit and vegetable skins, though they can also penetrate the inner flesh. They can overwork the liver and may also cause allergic skin reactions. Other fibre-rich foods include peas, beans of all kinds, lentils, oats, brown rice, buckwheat, and other unrefined grains.

HERBAL CLEANSERS

Certain herbs help to make the cleansing process more efficient. Burdock stimulates the liver; senna and yellow dock are mild laxatives; sarsaparilla cleans the kidneys and helps to re-balance the sex organs (imbalances often lie at the root of skin problems); and sassafras is a detoxifier which is particularly effective at cancelling out some of the injurious effects of cigarette smoke. These herbs can be taken either as infusions or in tablet form.

REPLENISHING

A good supply of nutrients is essential to make healthy new skin cells. But, sadly, it's not good enough simply to select foods that are packed with vitamins and minerals and then to hope for the best. Tension and emotional upsets all interfere with the digestion, so food is often only partially broken down, preventing nutrients being fully absorbed.

Always take time to unwind before sitting down to a meal – a glass of wine may help – and try to avoid eating hurried snacks, which upset the digestive system. If you suffer from indigestion, don't drink water just before or during a meal, as it dilutes the digestive enzymes, or try taking digestive enzyme supplements with your food.

Refined flour, which is used to make white bread, cakes, pastries and biscuits, contains gluten, which attaches itself to the intestinal wall, so hindering the absorption of available nutrients. Fibre-rich foods help to remove this substance, as can powdered psyllium husks. These come from the seeds of the plantain herb and swell in the stomach to absorb noxious substances and speed their removal from the body.

Significant amounts of B complex vitamins, which are vital for healthy skin, are made in the intestine by the bacteria that live there. The num-

- Each morning drink a cup of hot water mixed with the juice of half a lemon or grapefruit or a whole lime. Add some honey if desired.
- Drink as much spring or filtered water as you can. Aim to drink at least eight glasses daily.
- Replace tea and coffee with herbal teas. Rosehip is rich in vitamin C, while peppermint is refreshing and aids the digestion.
- Avoid fizzy and caffeine-laden drinks.
- If your complexion is blemished or dull, try a mini, two-day cleansing programme once a month where you should avoid processed foods, meat and dairy products and eat as many fresh, raw fruits and vegetables as possible.
- Cut down your intake of alcohol to a minimum. For example, don't drink more than two glasses of wine a day and avoid all spirits.
- Don't take antibiotics unless absolutely necessary, as they can destroy bacteria in the intestines. Help to counter-balance their effects with food supplying B complex vitamins and live yoghurt.
- Ensure that your diet is rich in natural high-fibre foods, such as fruits, vegetables, wholegrains and cereals.

ber of these organisms tends to dwindle in times of stress and illness, and when the diet contains too much meat, refined carbohydrates and sugars. Eating live, natural yoghurt helps to replenish these beneficial bacteria.

Opt for yoghurt made from goat's or sheep's milk rather than cow's, as this is easier to digest and less likely to provoke allergic reactions. If you cannot tolerate milk of any kind, it is possible to buy lactobacillus acidophilus bacteria (present in yoghurt) in tablet or capsule form.

SKIN SUPPLEMENTS

The B complex vitamins are needed for good circulation, which ensures that developing skin cells receive a good supply of nutrient-laden food and gets rid of unwanted wastes. Lack of B vitamins can result in redness, tenderness and other skin problems. Open pores and blackheads usually clear up when adequate amounts are present. Good sources include yeast extract, liver and wholegrain cereals.

Vitamin A is vital to the healthy manufacture

Keep the skin soft, smooth and blemish-free by following a regular cleansing routine.

of epidermal (superficial) skin cells. It also slows down the keratinisation, or hardening, of cells as they move to the uppermost layer, so making skin feel soft and smooth. A shortage causes dead, scaly cells to build up and block the pores, preventing oils from reaching the surface. The pores then become enlarged and can turn into unsightly blackheads or whiteheads.

Vitamin A abounds in fish liver oils. Carotene, a substance the body can convert into vitamin A, is found in orange-coloured fruits and vegetables, such as carrots, mangoes, cantaloupe melons, apricots and pumpkins, and in most green vegetables, egg yolk, liver, milk and butter.

The mineral zinc helps to transport vitamin A from the liver to the tissues. Research shows that skin conditions often improve when extra zinc is supplied. Along with zinc, the minerals magnesium, calcium and manganese all have to be present before proteins, which for a major proportion of cell material, can be constructed from the basic building blocks – amino acids. Large amounts of the trace

mineral sulphur crop up in the protein (keratin) of skin and hair, which is why it's often called the beauty mineral. Foods rich in sulphur include eggs, fish, onions and garlic.

Essential fatty acids are vital to healthy skin. The body uses them to construct the membranes surrounding each skin cell and, if these nutrients are lacking, the membranes weaken. This causes the skin to lose moisture and makes it susceptible to bacterial attack, which in turn encourages spots.

Essential fatty acids are found in oils extracted from olives, sunflower seeds, hazelnuts and sesame seeds. Within the body, their conversion to membrane-constructing fats can be blocked by a lack of vitamin C and zinc, or a diet that's loaded with animal fats and sugar. Evening primrose oil contains ready-converted essential fatty acids, so it makes a good supplement for skins that are excessively dry and flaky.

It takes a good three weeks for newly formed cells to reach the skin surface, so it takes time for lasting results to show. But soon after your cleansing regime starts, skin can soon begin to show some superficial improvement.

Skin care is a vital part of creating a clear complexion. So where do you start? There are three essentials in caring for your skin and, without these, it is unlikely that you will get the best results. Cleansing, toning and moisturising are the three basic steps that you need to follow and maintain a blemish-free, firm and radiant skin.

SKIN CLEAN

In a perfect world, skin would only need a splash of water to cleanse it efficiently. However, in reality, modern lifestyles take their toll on skin, and water is often just not enough to keep skin scrupulously clean. Environmental pollution, together with the make-up that we wear and the dead cells on the surface of our skin, can all contribute to making skin appear lacklustre and lifeless.

The solution? Improve your complexion by giving skin what it thrives on – regular attention. Some experts say that most of us should cleanse our faces twice a day – not more, as this may cause irritation – and deep cleanse our skin at least once a month.

Cleansing is the single most important aspect of skin care and for this reason a deep cleansing routine is an essential requirement if skin is to be kept in peak condition. There are a variety of basic cleansing products, each one with a specific method of application. Soap and water, liquid cleansers, cream cleansers, foaming gels, cleansing oils and cleansing pads are the main products available for basic skin cleansing. For deeper cleansing, facial scrubs, face masks and packs and steaming all remove dead skin cells from the skin's surface and remove any remaining pollutants.

LIQUID ASSETS

Soap and water is the most basic cleanser and for many skins it is not only the most effective, but the most refreshing cleanser to use too. However, choose your soap carefully. Many brands contain harsh detergents which work well for the body but tend to be too drying for the face. Soaps containing detergents strip the skin of its natural acid mantle, therefore disturbing the protective acid pH. This acid mantle protects the skin from harmful bacteria so look out for cleansing bars which are pH balanced and designed to cleanse without disrupting the skin's acidity.

Use moderately warm and not scalding water to wash your face. Work up a lather from the soap and use small circular movements to wash your face. Rinse with clean, warm water. If you wear an oil-based foundation, you may need to use an oil dissolving cream cleanser or a cleansing oil before you wash with a cleansing bar.

Cream or liquid cleansers are mainly oil-in-water emulsions which cleanse the skin by emulsifying water and oil-soluble grime. Massage into the skin and then remove with cotton wool, a tissue, or rinse off with water to wash away any traces of cleanser. Cream cleansers are more suitable for delicate, dry or mature skins, and are less suited to oily skins.

LATHER UP

Gels and foaming cleansers wash off, leaving the skin feeling fresh. Excellent for young or oily skins, they leave skin feeling thoroughly cleansed. Massage on to damp skin with the fingertips or use a cleansing brush, paying particular attention to the central panel (or T-zone) of the face, the forehead, nose and chin, where blemishes most often appear. Rinse with liberal splashes of warm water.

Lather up a foaming cleanser with a little warm water and a soft brush, to leave the skin feeling refreshed and deeply cleansed.

EXFOLIATORS AND FACIAL SCRUBS

Skin is constantly producing new cells and shedding old ones. In fact, a normal healthy skin renews itself totally every 28 days.

However, as we age, the process may slow down, leaving accumulated dead cells on the surface which give skin a rough texture and a dull appearance. Exfoliating products, such as facial scrubs, astringent lotions, alpha hydroxy acid-based preparations, abrasive pads and brushes, slough off any dead cells on the surface (the *stratum corneum*), leaving it smoother, more radiant and more even in colour. Basically, exfoliators work by abrading the surface of the skin, gently peeling away the discarded cells. Exfoliation also works on a deeper level by stimulating the skin's basal layer to produce new, fresh cells. This improves the superficial texture of the skin, again giving it a smoother surface, a more radiant glow and a more even skin tone. This is because the skin has literally been polished, and the cells on the surface are flat and smooth, refracting light and giving skin luminosity.

The latest breed of exfoliators contain alpha hydroxy acids (AHAs) which are derived from natural sources: glycolic acid comes from sugar cane; malic acid from apples; citric acid from citrus fruit and lactic acid from milk. Alpha hydroxy acids work by clearing away dead cells on the skin's surface, so making it appear smoother and more lustrous. Some AHAs, such as glycolic acid, are also thought to boost moisture levels by improving the skin's own water-binding function. Products containing AHAs are particularly useful for pepping up and stimulating older or tired skins but, like other exfoliators, they should not be used by those with overly sensitive or chapped skin as they may cause further irritation. Many dermatologists suggest that, if you use an exfoliator containing alpha hydroxy acids, you should take extra care when your skin is exposed to the sun and that it is best to use a sunscreen with a sun protection factor of at least 8.

Although some dermatologists recommend AHA-based preparations and abrasive scrubs for the treatment of severely oily skins or acne, they should be used in moderation and with extreme caution. If you have severe acne, consult a doctor or dermatologist before using any type of exfoliation treatment.

STEAM CLEAN

As a deep-cleansing treat, some beauticians recommend that you steam your face once in a while. Not only does a gentle steam help to cleanse skin, it also makes the skin more receptive to further treatment – in particular, before a facial massage or the application of a face mask. In addition, it opens the pores, encourages the elimination of ingrained impurities, relaxes muscle tissue and leaves skin feeling ultra clean. Steaming is a great way of cleansing oily to normal skin, but it is best avoided if your skin is sensitive or if you have a tendency to broken capillaries. If you don't have a facial sauna, use a bowl of cooling boiled water to which you have added a handful of herbs. Try sage or comfrey for delicate, dry skin, basil, mint or chamomile for oily skin and lavender or rose petals for normal skin. Hold your face about 8-10 inches above the bowl and cover your head with a towel. All you need is about 3 to 4 minutes of steam to cleanse thoroughly. Protect delicate areas such as around the eyes and the cheeks with a layer of moisturiser if skin is hyper-sensitive. When steaming is finished, pat the skin dry with a tissue.

DEEP CLEANSING FACE MASKS

Although dermatologists argue about the efficacy of face packs and masks for cleansing the skin, they have been used for centuries for their skin cleansing and healing properties. Many cleansing masks contain clay or mud which supposedly draws out and absorbs dirt and grime, while acting as a gentle exfoliant. Gel-based masks usually contain polymers which set to form a fine film and are then washed away with water to remove dead cells and stale make-up.

Sulphur-based masks are often used to treat acne and to control oily skin and should not be used on sensitive or dry skin, and winter green and menthol based masks help to increase the circulation and tighten pores. Apply your chosen mask to damp skin, ideally after steaming, and leave on for the specified time.

Masks are best painted on to the face with a brush. Take care to avoid the eye, nostril and lip areas, and remember that your neck will benefit as much as your face. Masks are usually left on the face for between 10 and 20 minutes, although the time does vary from product to product. When

Face masks help clean and revitalise the skin, and their benefits are well worth the extra effort and time they take.

Apply your mask to damp skin for the best effect. Steaming, either before or during, usually helps penetration.

removing the mask, be careful not to pull or drag the skin. Manufacturers may recommend their own removal method, but damp cotton wool is always good. If possible, apply your chosen mask while soaking in a warm bath as the steam will improve the results.

If you have time, make your own mask; for greasy skin, lightly beat an egg white, add lemon juice and mix with oatmeal. Leave for 10 minutes, then remove with cool water. For mature and acned skins mix wheatgerm (equally good for both skin types because of its vitamin E content) with oatmeal and milk to form a paste, leave for 15 minutes and rinse off. For dry skin mix avocado, apricot and banana into a pulp, then add sufficient cream to make a thick paste, or combine a tablespoon of fuller's earth and one of kelp. Leave for 30 minutes and rinse off.

MOISTURE

Whether or not most of us really need to use a moisturiser on our skins is a matter of great debate among dermatologists and cosmetologists. Not only does it depend on your skin type, but on the environment you live in. For example, if you have a dry skin and you are living in a hot climate or your skin is exposed regularly to the sun, then the chances are that you will probably need to use a moisturiser

both for comfort and to prevent flakiness and fine lines.

So what is moisturiser? Quite simply, it is a preparation that delivers water to the outer layers of the skin, creating a barrier against further water being lost. And how do they work? Moisturisers either produce an occlusive layer that helps to prevent water loss from the surface or they attract water from the surrounding environment. Some state-of-the-art moisturisers do both. The application of water to the surface of the skin plumps it up, as the *stratum corneum* absorbs the moisture, and the end result is an improved complexion. The further application of a moisturiser to dampened skin locks in the fluid and achieves an even better effect. Moisturisers are available in many forms from oil-in-water emulsions, which tend to be in lotion form, to water-in-oil emulsions, which are creams. Oil-in-water moisturisers are perfect for oily skins whereas water-in-oil moisturisers are best for dry and flaky complexions. It is best to have your skin analysed to determine your skin type, although it should be fairly obvious if you have very oily or dry skin. You can then choose the moisturiser that is best suited to your skin's needs. Although skin may change from season to season, in general its need for moisture is constant. Winter skin tends to need more moisture than summer skin, as warm air holds more moisture

SKIN CREAM INGREDIENTS

Although most dermatologists believe that no amount of hi-tech ingredients can really make any difference to the texture of our skin, cosmetic scientists beg to differ. Technically, ingredients that claim to alter the cellular structure of the skin (such as retinol) should really be classified as drugs and dermatologists believe that they should therefore be prescribed. The following ingredients are just a few of the most common substances that you may come across when buying a skin care preparation.

ADENOSINE TRIPHOSPHATE (ATP)
A molecule used to transfer energy from energy-yielding to energy-requiring cells. Used in some creams to boost cell metabolism and encourage regeneration.

ALLANTOIN
A natural substance which has healing and soothing properties. It is extracted from a water plant from the Conferva genus.

ALOE VERA
Extracted from the aloe vera cactus, this gel-like substance has been proven to have healing properties. Used for centuries by native Americans, it helps to reduce inflammation and alleviate painful skin conditions such as sunburn. Used in after-sun products.

ALPHA HYDROXY ACIDS (AHAs)
Also known as fruit acids, alpha hydroxy acids, are derived

from a variety of sources including grapes, milk, citrus fruits and apples. They literally sweep off the dead cells on the surface of the skin, leaving skin brighter and diminishing fine lines. They also supposedly increase the skin's moisture uptake. They are used in relatively small percentages in many over-the-counter skin creams and toning lotions. Dermatologists and beauty therapists, however, use them in higher concentrations in skin peels. They can cause a reaction in sensitive skins, so should be used with care and in moderation.

AMINO ACIDS
The building blocks of proteins and enzymes found in abundance in all skin cells. Also needed to make new collagen and elastin fibres which form the skin's support system. Vital for cell renewal. Also seem to play a role in binding moisture within the skin cells.

ANTIOXIDANTS
These include the vitamins A, C and E which are reported to have protective properties against cell damage caused by the action of free radicals (see Vitamin E).

AZULENE
Azulene is extracted from chamomile flowers. It acts as a desensitiser, and helps to protect skin from allergic reactions. It is most often used in face and body preparations and in cosmetics, to prevent allergy.

10-POINT SKIN WORKOUT

1. Start by removing any eye make-up with a gentle remover – oil-free removers are best. Apply the lotion to a cotton-wool pad and sweep it over the eyelid and lashes and under the eye. Always use a separate pad for each eye.

2. Remove any make-up by cleansing. Cleansing bars and foaming cleansers work well for most skin types. Splash skin with warm water and then apply the cleanser, massaging it into skin with circular movements. For blemish-prone skin, use a cleansing brush.

3. Use a facial exfoliator to remove dead skin cells. Massage on to damp skin, avoiding the delicate skin around the eyes and the mouth. Remove by rinsing with warm water.

4. Treat skin to reviving steam. Fill a large bowl with cooling, boiled water. Add herbs to the water, depending on your skin type. Hold your face about 25 cm (10 inches) away from the water and cover your head with a towel. Steam for three or four minutes.

5. Groom eyebrows and gently remove any blackheads.

6. Apply a deep-cleansing or moisturising mask. Apply for the specified amount of time, while relaxing in a warm bath or room. Remove and rinse thoroughly with warm water.

7. Tone skin to cleanse away any remaining traces of mask.

8. Apply a reviving serum to your fingertips and massage into the skin.

9. Apply a suitable moisturiser and massage it in.

10. Finish off by applying an eye gel or cream to alleviate any dryness around the eyes.

BEESWAX
Obtained from the honeycomb after the honey has been removed, it helps to smooth and soften the skin.

BISABOLOL
A calming chemical found in chamomile oil. It soothes inflammation and reduces redness, making it a popular ingredient in products geared to sensitive skins.

CAFFEINE
A mild stimulant, caffeine is an alkaloid drug which has minor diuretic and analgesic effects. It is used in skin care creams to stimulate blood circulation and lymphatic drainage – often found in body-contouring products and eye creams.

CERAMIDES
Waxy substances found naturally in the skin's intercellular cement – the glue that sticks scaly cells together in the protective *stratum corneum* (skin's surface layer). If the cement is eroded by washing or exposure to abrasive elements the barrier is weakened, leaving skin dry, and dull in appearance. Most modern creams, particularly those claiming to be anti-ageing or offering intensive moisturisation, contain ceramides to reinforce the intercellular cement.

CEREBROSIDES
Related to ceramides, they are found in creams which claim to restructure the skin, again by sticking together the skin's intercellular cement.

CLAY
A fine white powder obtained from sedimentary rock which includes kaolin, renowned for its purifying and absorbent properties. Often used in cleansing face masks.

COLLAGEN
A structural protein which is found in the connective tissue of the dermis, it is composed of protein fibres. It provides support and firmness to the skin. As we age, the fibres degenerate, resulting in loss of tone. Collagen is often broken down into amino acids before it is added to skin creams. It is claimed that it acts as a moisturiser and that it forms a protective, softening film over the skin.

GLUCIDS
A technical term for glucose and its derivatives. An energy source for the skin.

GLYCERIN
A chemical brew made by combining water and fat, which produces a transparent gel-like liquid. Glycerin helps to maintain the water content of moisturising products although when applied to the skin, it can actually absorb the skin's natural moisture. It is used in many face and body moisturisers.

HORSETAIL
The horsetail plant contains minerals which supposedly have a therapeutic effect on the skin's elasticity.

HYALURONIC ACID
One of the most widely acclaimed substances to be used in skin care, hyaluronic acid belongs to a family of gel-like substances known as mucopolysaccarides. It supposedly helps to absorb and hold water, making it a potent moisturiser.

LANOLIN
An oil extracted from sheep's wool, lanolin is similar in composition to the sebum of human skin. It acts as a moisture barrier on the surface of the skin, helping to trap water and keep skin soft and smooth. Lanolin has been shown to be a common allergen. It is used in moisturisers for face and body and in some cosmetics.

LINOLEIC AND GAMMA LINOLEIC ACID (GLA)
These are essential fatty acids, sometimes called vitamin F. They play a vital role in cell membranes, keeping them flexible and watertight. Lack of vitamin F results in dry, rough, itchy skin. Linoleic acids occur naturally in vegetable seed oils such as sunflower and safflower oils, while the rarer GLA is found in evening primrose and blackcurrant oils. Both are used in numerous moisturising creams and lotions.

LIPIDS
The skin's own sebaceous secretions are made up of lipids which form a lubricating and moisture-trapping film over the surface. Lipids in skin creams aim to replace and supplement these natural oils.

LIPOSOMES
Discovered by medical researchers, liposomes are tiny fatty microspheres which are used to transport and target active ingredients into the skin. They often contain moisturising or energising substances. Because of their microscopic dimensions, they apparently pass through the skin's surface cells and carry the active ingredients to the deeper layers where they react with the skin's own chemicals, disperse and release their contents.

NATURAL MOISTURISING FACTOR (NMF)
The skin's natural moisturising factor, NMF, can be extracted and used to maintain moisture levels on the skin's surface. Used in moisturisers.

OLIGO ELEMENTS
Trace minerals essential to the functioning of enzymes involved in making healthy new cells.

OXYGEN
Used as a vehicle or transport system in anti-ageing skin creams. It is claimed that oxygen helps to carry moisture (water) and other active ingredients into the epidermis.

PANTHENOL
A derivative of vitamin B5, (pantothenic acid) that helps bolster the skin's natural resilience, calm sensitivity and protect skin against environmental hazards. Often used in mascara and in nail treatments, it supposedly strengthens nails and lashes.

PHOSPHOLIPIDS
These play a major role in the structure of cell membranes. These membranes regulate the flow of nutrients (including oxygen) into, and wastes out of, the cells.

PLANT EXTRACTS
These have numerous qualities. They can help to firm up (hops) and tighten tissue (red vine, horse chestnut), calm (chamomile) and boost circulation (ivy). Often used in products designed to refine and firm up puffy or flabby tissue on hips and thighs.

POLYMER
A natural derivative obtained from cellulose, a constituent of plant tissues. It has moisture absorbing and retaining properties. Used in intensive moisturising skin creams and masks and in hair products.

PYROLIDONE CARBOXYLIC ACID (PCA)
A constituent of the skin's NMF, it provides the skin with substances essential for restoring moisture balance. Used in moisturisers.

RETINYL PALMITATE
A relation of vitamin A, this ingredient is often used in anti-ageing creams. Cosmetic scientists claim that it has a mild regenerating effect on the skin. However, there is no evidence that the small amounts of retinyl palmitate used in skin-care creams have much effect.

TYROSINE
A natural amino acid which is present in skin cells, Tyrosine is converted into the tanning pigment melanin when skin is exposed to sunlight. It is used in pre-tan products to help stimulate natural levels. It is claimed that it helps to speed up tanning and protect skin from UVA and UVB rays.

VEGETABLE OILS
These form a fine protective film over the skin (similar to the skin's own oily secretions) and so seal in moisture to keep skin soft and supple.

VITAMIN E (TOCOPHEROL)
Known as the anti-ageing vitamin, vitamin E is a natural anti-oxidant which helps to protect the body's cells from the destructive and ageing effects of free radicals, marauding chemicals within the body. It works by protecting polyunsaturated fats, such as linoleic acid from the free radicals, which can be activated by ultra violet light, pollution, and toxins including cigarette smoke and alcohol.

WITCH HAZEL
A North American shrub which has been used for centuries to heal and tone the skin and as a wash for the eyes. Its firming and astringent properties make it a useful ingredient in skin toners and cleansers.

XANTHINES
Chemical relatives of caffeine, xanthines are often used in anti-cellulite preparations. In particular, Aminophylline, a xanthine, is believed to speed up fat burning, so helping to eliminate fatty deposits on thighs, upper arms and buttocks.

than cold, but this doesn't mean that you can forget about moisturising during the summer months. The low humidity of hot climates and the dehydrating effects of sunlight, air-conditioning and chemically treated water, all cause moisture loss in the summer and central heating and harsh winter weather can dehydrate skin during the winter months. The use of soaps and detergents can also affect the skin's moisture balance and can cause dehydration by stripping away the skin's protective lipid layer.

Other factors, such as hormonal changes or the ageing process, may also affect your skin's moisture requirements. For example, some women find that their skin texture changes before and during menstruation and that they need to use less moisturiser. And as we grow older, the protective film or lipid layer on the surface of the skin becomes less effective giving poorer protection against water loss, leading to dry, flaky skin that demands the use of a moisturiser.

Dermatologists also believe that skin has a natural moisturising factor (NMF) which helps to regulate water flow from the depths of the dermis to the epidermis or surface of the skin. The NMF decreases with age, so increasing the need for a moisturiser containing water-regulating ingredients.

Apart from water and NMF, sebum plays an important role in preventing moisture loss by creating an occlusive layer on the surface of the skin which delays water evaporation. That doesn't mean, however, that if you have an oily skin you don't need to use a moisturiser. You may have plenty of oil but not enough water and your skin can become rough in texture and may feel taught and uncomfortable. If you do have an oily complexion, opt for an oil-free product which will deliver moisture without leaving your skin feeling greasy.

EYE CONTACT

The eyes are the windows to the souls and need to be treated with some respect. The area around the eyes is the first to show the visible signs of ageing. The skin here is finer and has fewer sebaceous glands to create moisture-retaining sebum.

Energy and vitality also reveal themselves in clear eyes. Too many late nights and the strain of overwork will dull their sparkle. Dark shadows under the eyes can be a sign of bad blood circulation and accumulated toxins due to a sluggish lymphatic system. So, first of all, improve your health by taking more exercise, preferably in the open air. This will boost your circulation, which can also too easily become sluggish in the winter, and may help to dispel any accumulated toxins.

Next, check your diet. Shortages of essential nutrients can sap energy. Low iron is often linked with listlessness, so up your iron intake with natural sources such as liver, wheatgerm, lentils, parsley and cereals. In order to absorb and use iron, the body needs vitamin C. Bioflavonoids (referred to by some as vitamin P) have been found to accompany vitamin C in fruit and vegetables and it is believed that they play a helpful role in maintaining healthy blood vessels. A properly balanced, nutritious diet must include plenty of these foods.

Puffiness and redness can be caused by excess alcohol and smoking. Cut down on both, cleanse the digestive system by drinking lots of lemon juice and water, and get plenty of sleep. Vitamin B complex and C tablets can help replace the nutrients that are killed by smoking and drinking.

Herbal tea bags used as compresses bring comfort to smoke-smitten eyes and reduce puffiness and shadows. Elderflower calms redness, peppermint cools and brightens, while chamomile soothes irritation. Dip herbal tea bags in hot water, squeeze to remove the excess liquid, and place on the lids for 10 minutes. Cotton wool soaked in witch-hazel reduces swelling. Eye make-up removers with the same pH as tears, and therapeutic plant extracts, such as cornflower and rosewater, are also highly beneficial.

In addition, ensure that you care for the skin around your eyes with a moisturising cream designed especially for this sensitive area. It is best to choose gels and creams that are oil- and fragrance-free. The simpler the formula, the less likely it is to irritate the eyes. Pat a few dots of eye cream on to the lids and underneath the eyes and massage in very gently with the fingertips, using small circular movements.

BODYWORKS
TOP TO TOE MAINTENANCE

Just as our faces need constant attention, so the skin covering the rest of our body also deserves to be treated with care. The hands and feet are constantly abused by extreme temperatures, while the arms, legs and breasts all need regular restorative treatments.

Poor circulation is the root of some of our most common skin complaints, especially during the winter months. Cold feet and hands, chilblains, dull skin and cellulite are all linked to sluggish blood flow. Poor circulation tends to be inherited, but the problem is often exacerbated by climate and lifestyle.

Skin glows when blood flows freely through tiny capillaries lying close to the surface. This explains why people with poor circulation often have pallid complexions. When skin is cold, the trouble worsens. To reduce heat loss, these vessels contract to prevent blood reaching the surface. Further attempts to conserve warmth also result in blood being channelled away from the extremities – hence the all-too-common problem of cold hands and feet in winter.

Vigorous exercise is one of the best ways to generate heat in the body and redirect blood back to the skin and extremities. Brisk walking, running and swimming help re-establish good circulation in all areas of the body. Emotional tension results in tight muscles, which interfere with the flow of blood. Gentle stretching exercises can relieve this.

Other techniques can be used to stimulate circulation in specific problem areas – for example, on upper thighs. Brush the skin briskly with a loofah or natural bristle body brush, dipped in cold water. Rub dry with a warm towel. After a warm bath, spray hips, thighs and bottom with cool then warm water, then finish with cool again.

Massage mitts with specially moulded surfaces help to stimulate circulation at a deeper level and are reputed to help disperse fat cells, too. For maximum effect, these mitts should be used in conjunction with a cream containing plant extracts that help encourage blood flow to the skin's surface.

Circulation may also be improved from within. Certain nutrients are believed to influence the state of the capillaries and vessels through which blood travels. The most documented is vitamin B3, rich sources of which are found in poultry, fish, brewer's yeast, wheatgerm, peanuts and liver.

Vitamin E can help, too. It occurs naturally in

Achieve the body beautiful and improve skin tone and condition with stimulating body treatments.

all grains, nuts and seeds. Vegetable oils contain large quantities, but it is destroyed by cooking and processing. Vitamin C and the bioflavonoids may also help to strengthen weak capillaries. They are found together in berries, citrus fruits and peppers. It may be a good idea to take a daily supplement of between 500 and 1,000 mg of vitamin C in the colder, winter months.

With a combination of exercise, a nutritious, well-balanced diet and massage, you can achieve quick and effective body-shaping results. Healthy eating is an essential element of body shaping. Although crash diets will neither shift stubborn fat cells on thighs, hips and bottom nor alleviate cellulite, research has shown that, by modifying your diet, you can actually lessen the build-up of toxins and thus improve the circulation.

Take preventative measures against cellulite by cutting down on carbohydrates, processed and pre-cooked foods, alcohol and caffeine. Increase your intake of fresh and unsweetened vegetable and fruit juices, mineral water and herbal teas. Vitamin C is an efficient detoxifier and is found in citrus and berry fruits and in green vegetables, such as broccoli and spinach.

Vitamin E is also thought to be beneficial because it stimulates the circulation, and recent research points to vitamin B3 as an essential nutrient for the prevention of cellulite.

Get to grips with body buffing to create a smoother silhouette. Use a natural bristle brush or hemp mitt to stimulate your blood circulation and encourage the elimination of toxins via the lymphatic system, so helping to break down fatty pockets of cellulite. With long, upward, sweeping movements, start at the feet and work up the legs and across the hips and bottom. If you have sensitive skin, use a mitt and soap while showering, as water will minimise damage by decreasing friction. Don't pummel your thighs too hard or you could break capillaries and cause bruising. For body brushing to have any effect, you must, ideally, do it twice daily. Use a firm hand to brush up on your massage technique.

Professional massages are most effective for toning the skin, but you can easily do it yourself at home and achieve good results. After a warm shower or bath, begin your massage with *effleurage* – long, upward strokes that stimulate circulation and lymphatic drainage. Work your way up from your feet to your thighs and bottom. Follow this with *pétrissage* – a technique that consists of squeezing and rolling the muscles. Use firm movements and squeeze the flesh between fingers and thumb as if kneading dough. Finish with *tapotement* – slapping and chopping movements that aid muscle tone and skin firmness. Use massage oils to help the hands glide across the skin.

HAND FEEDING

Cold weather, sunlight, soap suds and strong detergents wear away the lipid film that protects skin from moisture loss, leaving hands feeling dry and rough. Start treating from within. Diets rich in vitamins A, B complex and E nourish the skin, while some minerals, such as zinc, calcium, magnesium and iodine, help nails grow long and strong. Also treat hands and nails to a thorough workout. Massage hands with a rich night cream for five minutes every evening to moisturise parched cells. After a generous application of hand cream at night, wear a pair of cotton gloves in bed to keep the moisture close to the skin.

Whenever possible, wear gloves to protect your hands and nails, especially when doing housework and gardening, both of which can do damage almost beyond repair. During the daytime, select a cream or lotion containing ultraviolet filters that protect skin from harmful, ageing rays.

NAIL FILE

Neglect nails at your peril. Nails can dry out and become brittle, making them prone to splitting and peeling, so smother them in creams designed to moisturise and protect. Regular manicures are essential to keep nails healthy. Treat yourself to a weekly manicure by following this simple regime.

1. Remove any polish. Soak fingers in warm water with lemon juice. For extremely dry hands, soak fingers in warm oil, such as almond oil. Dry the fingers and clean away loosened dirt with an orange stick, without prodding under the nail.

2. Rub cuticle cream into each nail and massage with firm, circular movements of the thumb. This encourages the underlying 'embryo' nail to grow, keeps nails pliable and boosts circulation. Now ease back the cuticle with an orange stick.

3. Shape nails with extra care. Trim with sharp

Slough away rough dead skin with a pumice stone or loofah to leave the skin smooth and supple.

scissors or nail-clippers, then shape with an emery board, moving it in one direction only and filing from the centre to the side of the nail. After shaping, nails may be dry. Dip into almond oil and wipe with a tissue.

4. For a natural, healthy sheen, buff nails with a chamois buffer.

5. To give shine to dull nails, use a coat of clear base. Strengthen and give shine to dull, brittle nails with clear base coats and nail protectors as part of your weekly manicure .

DO-IT-YOURSELF PEDICURE

Feet are often neglected. Hidden away during winter months under layers of socks, or squashed into boots or shoes all year round, they need special attention to revive them.

Soften hardened skin and relax hot, tired feet by soaking them for 15 minutes in a basin of comfortably hot water, adding a few drops of almond or apricot kernel oil. Essential oils make a footbath uplifting or relaxing and leave feet smelling sweet. Good aromatherapy oils include geranium, orange, lavender, rosemary, peppermint, camphor and tangerine.

THE ROUGH WITH THE SMOOTH

Hard, calloused skin can build up on neglected feet, so exfoliate them regularly to promote smooth skin. After soaking, slough away hard skin with a pumice stone or bristle brush. Kneading and rubbing feet not only relieves aches, it also helps relax the mind. If your feet tend to feel cold, regular massage will help improve blood circulation. A good foot massage also helps dispel the day's tension. Massage with sweeping movements from the toes to the ankle. Use a soothing and moisturising lotion or cream and rub into toes, soles and the tops of the feet.

Treat your toenails with the same care as you would your fingernails. Use a cuticle cream to soften the cuticles and push them back with an orange stick. Trim your toenails straight across and file away any rough edges. It helps if you separate your toes during your pedicure with cotton-wool balls or rolled-up tissues.

BREASTS AND DECOLLETE

Smooth, soft skin is not just a prerequisite for summer beauty – it's an essential all year round. Shoulders, arms, back and neck need special attention to ensure that the skin has a perfect, polished finish. Body-buffers help to exfoliate the surface of the skin, leaving it gleaming and silken smooth. Exfoliation removes dead cells, grime and oily residues on the skin by gentle friction, by means either of rough mitts or granular scrubs. Skin naturally sheds these cells, but the process is slowed down by wearing foundation or face or body creams.

To keep normal and oily skin in peak condition, use an exfoliator weekly; dry skin may benefit from a bi-weekly treatment. Loofah, hemp mitts and synthetic fibre sponges can be used to buff the skin on their own. Use on warm, damp skin – ideally in the bath or shower – and rub gently with sweeping, upward strokes and circular movements, taking care not to irritate the skin.

SIMPLE SCRUBS

It's easy to make your own scrubs using simple ingredients, readily found in most kitchens. A basic but effective scrub can be made by mixing a handful each of ground oatmeal, almonds and bran with rose or orange flower water. Rub the mixture over damp skin and wash off with warm water. Or blend two tablespoons of natural yoghurt, one tablespoon of grated citrus peel, one tablespoon of oatmeal flakes and two tablespoons of wheatgerm oil or light vegetable oil, and make a paste that can be rubbed on to the skin and massaged in with circular movements.

For an invigorating salt-based scrub, blend half a cup of warmed milk with a tablespoon of honey and stir in. Add a quarter of a cup of table salt and 10 drops of essential oil of peppermint or tangerine for a cooling body scrub. Rinse thoroughly with warm water and take care to avoid any contact with the eyes. After exfoliating, smooth on body cream or lotion to help protect the skin and to leave it soft, supple and lightly perfumed. Sensitive skin may benefit from a cream-based granular scrub.

WORKING OUT

Probably the single most effective means of improving the appearance of the bust is exercise. Although the breast itself contains no muscle, it is supported by the pectoral muscles, which are attached to the chest, and by the weaker muscles of the neck, which fan out across the decolleté. When these are well toned, the breasts are held firmly in place. When they are neglected, they deteriorate and allow the bust to sag.

A bra, of course, holds the breasts in place, but it also renders the muscles redundant. But be warned – gravity is even more damaging. With the exception of the virtually flat-chested, no one should abandon wearing a bra, but should embark instead on a few exercises to counteract its effect. Incorporate five to 10 minutes, three or four times a week, into your daily exercise programme to keep these muscles strong.

Hydrotherapy is an excellent bust firmer and toner. Water treatments stimulate blood flow and tighten the skin but, as such effects are transient, regular spraying with cold water is vital. When you shower, spray the breasts first with warm water, then with cold. Alternate each for 30 seconds for a couple of minutes each day.

Massage is also beneficial in keeping the breasts firm and toned. Use a bland oil such as coconut to massage breasts. For a stimulating effect, add a few drops of essential oil of peppermint. Always protect the nipples from the effects of the sun and use a little cocoa butter to keep them soft and supple.

BUST WORKOUT

1. Press your hands together in front of your chest, prayer fashion, and push as hard as possible for 10 seconds.

2. Hold your arms out to the sides at shoulder height, with fists clenched, and circle forwards 10 times, then backwards 10 times.

3. Adopt the press-up position. Bend your arms slightly to lower the body (not all the way to the ground) and straighten them again. Do this 10 times.

4. When swimming, do the breaststroke; water offers beneficial resistance. Cold water tightens the tissues. Hot water does the opposite.

5. Grimace by clenching the lower jaw to work the neck muscles.

SKIN AGEING
HOLDING BACK THE YEARS

Why does skin age? Do sunlight, pollution, smoking and alcohol really accelerate the ageing process? Can we stop the biological clock ticking away? The most vulnerable organ of the body, skin is exposed to both internal and external attack. The latest scientific evidence has proved that environmental hazards are responsible for speeding up natural ageing. But the good news is that we can combat premature ageing by guarding skin from both within and without.

Ageing is one of the most complex biological processes that the body has to contend with. There are a number of theories that explain how and why our skin ages but most dermatologists now believe that ultraviolet light, in particular UVA, is mainly responsible for speeding up the process. As we age, our body loses its ability to adapt to environmental changes as quickly as it should to give us adequate protection. Skin ageing also depends very much on individual genetic inheritance and, consequently, some skins age more quickly than others.

Ageing skin goes through a number of biological changes. Cell division and cell growth become impaired. Blood circulation becomes poorer, the essential water content decreases and the visible changes that are associated with skin ageing gradually become apparent. The appearance of wrinkles and lines is often the first sign.

Elasticity and firmness are lost slowly but surely and the texture can change, with the appearance of uneven areas of dry, flaky skin. Skin also becomes thinner and more transparent, losing much of its protective power. Pigmentation is affected too with the formation of patchy, light and dark areas, especially on sun-exposed skin. The ageing process in the skin is not different from what takes place elsewhere in the body, but it can happen faster and be accelerated because it is exposed to both internal and external attack. Skin ageing starts on a cellular level with changes in the genetic DNA and RNA within the cells.

Natural ageing – that is, the ageing that occurs simply because the biological clock is ticking away – is not reversible, other than by major forms of surgery, such as face-lifts. But much of the visible signs of ageing can be attributed to sun damage, not natural ageing. Dermatologists cite the comparison between sun-exposed skin on the face or hands with skin which is seldom exposed, such as the buttocks or undersides of the arm, to prove that the sun wreaks havoc. Skin that is almost constantly protected looks smoother, has fewer lines and is generally firmer to touch. However, the face is the most expressive part of the body and many of the deeper surface lines are undoubtedly caused by the daily wear and tear brought on by laughing, frowning and general stress. Apart from the superficial changes that occur on the surface, complex chemical reactions deep down in the dermis and the epidermis modify the very structure of the skin, causing major alterations.

But why do these changes occur? According to many scientists, free radicals – marauding particles formed by complex chemical reactions – are responsible for much of the damage that is done to skin. Free radicals are highly reactive molecular groups that combine with DNA enzymes or cell membranes, causing damage, particularly to the chromosomes, and so distorting the genetic blueprint of the cell.

Free radicals are produced by the interaction of oxygen with polyunsaturated fats, which then form semi-stable peroxides capable of destroying proteins in the body. The main protein, DNA, can be irreparably damaged by free radicals and damage is also caused to the skin's lipids, cell membranes and collagen. When a cell is damaged by free radicals, the result is known as a lipofuscin pigment granule, or 'clinker'. The greater the damage and the more clinkers that are formed, the older the skin appears, as they result in mottled pigmentation, wrinkles and loss of elasticity. Free radicals are also formed when ultraviolet radiation penetrates into a cell membrane – another good reason to avoid sunbeds and excessive sun exposure. The good news is that you can protect yourself from some of this damage by ensuring that you control levels of stress, have regular exercise, protect your body from harsh environmental elements and eat a diet rich in anti-oxidants, which are chemicals that soak up the reactive energy of free radicals, thereby helping to slow down the ageing process.

IMPORTANT VITAMINS

Start by increasing your intake of the vitamins A, B, C and E, all of which are, according to the latest medical research, potent anti-oxidants. Vitamin A is thought to be a powerful anti-ageing vitamin. It stimulates the thymus gland, which controls the immune system, and helps to improve the texture and quality of skin.

Vitamins B1, B2, B3, B5, B6, B12 and folic acid are all vital to maintaining a healthy immune system and are useful anti-oxidants. In particular, B6 is thought to be essential for the healthy formation of collagen.

Vitamin C is an important anti-oxidant, which plays a significant role in maintaining the immune system. Recent research has revealed that vitamin C can detoxify harmful heavy metals, such as iron, cadmium and lead, and protects us from environmental pollutants. The level of vitamin C in the blood plasma of smokers, heavy alcohol drinkers, and those over the age of 60 is low, so it is particularly important for these groups to ensure that their diet is rich in this vitamin. The regular use of drugs, including aspirin, the Pill and antibiotics, increases the body's need for vitamin C.

Vitamin E is a powerful free radical scavenger. It helps to neutralise the harmful effects of unsaturated fats in the body and prevents the formation of harmful peroxides. Research also shows that vitamin E can protect against irradiation, which itself causes the synthesis of free radicals in the cells. As vitamin E cannot be synthesised by the body, it is important to ensure that we get sufficient quantities through our diet.

AGEING ULTRAVIOLET

There is no doubt that sun damages the skin, often beyond repair. Scientists now believe that UVA is the ray most likely to speed up the ageing process and could, indeed, be the ray linked with skin cancer. UVA has the longest wavelength and penetrates deep into the dermis, where it not only causes the formation of free radicals, but also interferes with the natural production of collagen and elastin.

This is known as photoageing. Dermatologists are now suggesting that if we use broad spectrum sun protection whenever we sunbathe and a product with a low sunscreen daily, whenever we are outdoors, we can dramatically reduce the rate at which our skin ages. The repeated use of sunbeds is obviously not a wise idea. Sunbeds give out concentrated UVA radiation, which penetrates deep into the dermis, causing untold damage. If you must use a sunbed, use it in moderation, but experts believe that abstinence is advisable.

The only way to protect ourselves against ultraviolet-induced ageing, or photoageing, is to ensure that our skin is always properly protected.

Always use a protective moisturiser if you are outdoors during the day. Even if it is cloudy, those harmful UV rays manage to penetrate and do their damage. And take proper precautions when sunbathing or whenever skin is exposed to strong sunlight, especially when abroad. (See Chapter 8 on Sun Protection.)

AGEING ACCELERATORS

SMOKING

There is no doubt that smoking accelerates the ageing process. Smoking inhibits cell respiration and slows down the circulation, by constricting the blood vessels. This depletes the exchange of nutrients to the skin cells and inhibits the elimination of waste products. Cigarette smoke also releases a chemical called benzopyrine, which destroys ascorbic acid – vitamin C. In turn, a lack of vitamin C slows down the production of collagen, thereby contributing to premature wrinkles.

ALCOHOL

Alcohol produces acetaldehyde, which is usually converted to acetate in the liver and excreted. However, if the liver has been damaged by excess intake of alcohol, acetaldehyde is absorbed in the body where it encourages cross-linking of cells, which can lead to the formation of free radicals. In addition, alcohol depletes the body's vitamin reserves, especially of B complex and C. It is also dehydrating, reducing the levels of moisture in the skin and leading to dryness. Too much alcohol can dilate the blood vessels, especially in the face, and cause redness – broken or dilated capillaries can also appear permanently.

ENVIRONMENTAL STRESS

Dramatic changes in temperature, harsh chemicals such as detergents and soaps, central heating and air conditioning can all take their toll on skin and encourage premature ageing. More harmful are the environmental pollutants, such as lead, cadmium, aluminium and mercury, which can accumulate in the body and encourage the formation of dangerous peroxides which, in turn, attack cell protein. Take action and protect yourself with a diet rich in anti-oxidants, including vitamins C and E, the minerals selenium, zinc and iron, pectin and seaweed, all of which help to detoxify and eliminate harmful pollutants. (See Chapter 1.)

ANTI-AGEING PROGRAMME

● **Always wear a protective moisturiser when your skin is exposed to the elements. Look out for moisturisers that contain UV filters, especially UVA screens, to protect skin from the effects of photoageing.**
● **Ensure that the delicate skin around the eyes is protected, especially when skin is exposed to extremes in temperature. Use the fingertips to tap on a special moisturising cream around the eyes in a gentle circular motion.**
● **Wear gloves to protect the hands during the winter months and always apply a layer of hand cream containing a sunscreen before venturing outdoors. Massage cream into the fingertips and rub well into the palms, backs of the hands and wrists.**
● **Avoid the use of detergent soap to cleanse skin. Instead, look out for non-detergent cleansing bars and foaming cleansers or use liquid or creamy cleansers if your skin is very dry. Detergents tend to deplete the skin's natural moisture levels and are best avoided.**
● **Replenish lost moisture by using a rich hydrating mask at least once a week during winter. Apply to damp skin and leave on for at least 15 minutes, preferably while soaking in a warm bath.**
● **Always wear a high-protection sunscreen when skin is exposed to strong sunlight. Avoid the use of sunbeds. Wear sunglasses to protect the delicate skin around the eyes.**

THE AGES OF SKIN

From our teenage years onwards, our skin goes through numerous biological and physiological changes that effect its structure and appearance.

TWENTIES

While your skin goes through major changes in your teens, it usually settles down in your twenties. It is elastic, quick to heal, and the outer layer, the epidermis, renews itself every 28 days. You should have few wrinkles, and any that you do have will probably be around the eyes. Resilient collagen and elastin fibres ensure that your skin is supple and toned and a thin padding of fat beneath the dermis gives skin a healthy plumpness. In your early twenties, hormones are still stabilising, so you may experience periods of oiliness or have occasional blemishes. By the time you're 25, the hormones should be properly balanced.

If you sunbathed carelessly in your teens or were exposed to strong sunlight when you were a young child, damage to the blueprint of your cells will already have been done. To prevent further damage, always use a protective sunscreen whenever you are in strong sunlight. Skin could also benefit from the daily use of a moisturiser containing a low-level sunfilter.

Always keep skin hydrated with a suitable moisturiser. Avoid smoking and keep your alcohol intake to two glasses of wine per day. Drink plenty of still spring water and replace tea and coffee with herbal tisanes. Keep saturated fats to a minimum and eat a diet rich in fresh fruit and vegetables, avoiding processed foods whenever possible.

THIRTIES

Lines and wrinkles will become more apparent in your thirties. Pigmentation will also begin to change, as skin cells become less efficient at manufacturing the melanin that gives skin its colour. Skin tone often becomes uneven and patchy, especially on the chest, neck and face. If you have sunbathed without taking proper precautions, the collagen that keeps skin elastic will have been irreparably damaged and skin elasticity will be reduced.

The lines around your eyes and mouth will become more prominent and sebum production will decrease, so skin will need more moisture. It may also benefit from regular treatment with serums and intensive anti-ageing products. Take

particular care when exposed to the sun and use a high-protection sunscreen when sunbathing.

FORTIES

Now the gradual changes of ageing will be more obvious. Surface lines are deeper, especially the laughter lines around the mouth and the lines around the eyes. This is due to skin losing its elasticity and changes in collagen.

Pigmentation will be noticeably uneven, unless you have avoided the sun. There may be dark spots of sun damage beside lighter areas due to the changes in the production of melanin. Your skin will produce very little sebum and you will need to use a heavier moisturiser. It is essential that you take precautions when in the sun to avoid skin cancer and that you avoid smoking, alcohol and a diet rich in fats.

Because the circulation is also slowing down, it is important take regular exercise and stimulate blood flow with regular self-massage and body brushing, which also acts on the lymphatic system.

FIFTIES PLUS

Lines and wrinkles will be more pronounced and it is unlikely that any skin product will be able to reduce them. However, the regular use of a high-performance moisturiser will help skin to retain moisture more efficiently and will keep skin looking plump and smooth. It is essential that you avoid the sun at all costs, so use a high-protection sunscreen when outdoors in strong sunlight. Regular exercise and massage will boost your circulation and encourage blood flow, so helping to nourish and cleanse the skin from within.

ANTI-AGEING SKIN CARE

There is no skin cream, or indeed drug, powerful enough to reverse the ageing process. The latest technological advances in cosmetics, however, claim to help retard it. Now that dermatologists have established the distinction between natural ageing and photoageing, progress is being made in the eternal quest for an anti-ageing product. Recent discoveries in the cosmetic laboratories owe much to medical science and this cross-over has lead to a revolution in skin care.

RETIN-A

A powerful drug rather than a cosmetic, researchers claim that it is the most authentic anti-ageing preparation science has discovered, although it appears to be effective only for the treatment of sun-aged skin. An acne treatment that has been in use for 20 years, Retin-A, or tretinoin, is one of 2,000 synthetic retinoids that derive from vitamin A.

So how does Retin-A repair sun-aged skin and reduce wrinkles?

It has been proved that retinoids speed up new cell production and old cell turnover, help to restructure disorderly, pre-cancerous cells, and increase the amount of intercellular mucus that prevents cells clumping together, so allowing them to be shed normally.

The most recent proof of the power of Retin-A comes from intensive testing carried out by Dr John Voorhees at the University of Michigan Medical School. A four-month study of 30 men and women aged between 35 and 70, all of whom had varying degrees of sun-aged skin, showed that Retin-A reduced sun-induced lines, produced rapid cell turnover, created a smoother skin surface and decreased wrinkles.

This backs up early reports by Dr Albert Kligman, American doyen of dermatology and director of the Ageing Skin Clinic at the University of Pennsylvania, who was responsible for the original development of Retin-A for acne treatment. Kligman reported improvements in skin smoothness of mature acne patients using the drug over long periods.

Dr Voorhees does not, however, recommend it is used without substantial reason because it does have its drawbacks. Side-effects associated with its use include scaly, rough and inflamed skin, and uncomfortable sensations of itching and burning during the first eight to 10 weeks of use. The cream thins the skin's outermost layer, making it hypersensitive to sun damage and liable to skin cancer caused by UV light.

While using Retin-A, it is imperative that a sunscreen of at least SPF 15 is used daily and tanning avoided altogether. It has been suggested by some doctors that Retin-A is also teratogenic and, as such, could cause birth defects in the foetus of a pregnant woman using the cream. However, this claim is refuted by Kligman and Voorhees, who have seen no evidence of this in 20 years of work with Retin-A. At present, Retin-A is available in the UK only on prescription. In the US, however, dermatologists are already prescribing it for those with sun-damaged skin.

MICROSCOPE

It may be years before the safety of Retina-A is fully established so, in the meantime, we can best prevent photoageing by protecting our skin with effective sunscreens. In the realm of cosmetics, scientists have been inspired by medical discoveries, such as that of Retin-A, to investigate the possibilities of anti-ageing skin creams.

The secret of many of these new creams is microencapsulation. The first microcapsule to be discovered was the liposome in 1961, now widely used in both medicine and cosmetics. Liposomes are fluid-filled lipid spheres made up of fatty molecules called phospholipids. These microscopic balloons are now being used in medicine for drug dispersal as they can be filled with a variety of medications and can be used without fear of disturbing the body's natural mechanisms.

Scientists claim that, because of their microscopic size, liposomes can penetrate the epidermis, becoming effective vehicles for active ingredients that will encourage cell renewal and turnover and thereby giving skin a smoother, plumper appearance. Leading cosmetic companies have been quick to apply liposome technology to new ranges of products that, in different ways, promise to revitalise the complexion. Microencapsulation can be enhanced by the addition of certain vitamins known to be active in skin repair. Lipids and ceramides are also being added to some creams to help retain moisture.

SURFACE BENEFITS

Another area in the search for an anti-ageing product in which medicine and beauty have crossed paths is that of transdermal delivery. This method of transportation was pioneered by medical research but is now being borrowed by the cosmetic industry.

Sticking plasters are applied to the surface of the skin in order to introduce drugs into the bloodstream. Transdermal patches are an improvement on orally taken pills because they do not have to be metabolised by the liver, which means that smaller, safer doses can be used. In America, cosmetics using transdermal delivery technology have already been created. Skin patches to moisturise, firm and tone the skin have been produced by one leading pharmaceutical company. Could this be the skin care of the future?

CHAPTER SIX

HAIR

The condition and appearance of hair, like that of skin, is a gauge of inner health. Nothing is more admired than a full head of glossy, healthy tresses, regardless of colour or length. Yet many people neglect their hair – subject it to daily damage and then wonder why it refuses to behave. Stress, poor diet, hormonal imbalance and simple maltreatment can quickly result in dull-looking hair, split ends and, at worst, hair loss. Brush up on your hair care and bring a shine to lacklustre locks.

CROWNING GLORY
HAIR HEALTH, CARE AND REPAIR

Hair has always been regarded as a focus of attention. Our crowning glory, hair changes according to age, occupation, health and environment. Like skin, it is also a barometer of our inner health and is vulnerable to the stresses and strains of modern lifestyles. Long or short, straight or curly, hair needs constant care and attention to keep it in peak condition.

Hair is composed of strong, elastic strands of protein, called keratin, which are a chemical blend of elements, including oxygen, iron, nitrogen, hydrogen, sulphur, carbon and phosphorus. It is made up of three different layers – the cuticle, the cortex and the medulla. The cuticle, which is the outer layer, has a scaly, horny surface, which helps to protect the inner layers from external damage, although it is soft enough to allow the penetration of chemicals used to colour and perm hair.

The cortex is the second layer and is considered to be the most important part of the hair structure. Controlling such essential qualities as elasticity, growth patterns and texture, the cortex is formed by millions of hard keratin fibres placed in a parallel position, and sometimes interwoven like a rope. The cortex also holds the key to the colour of your hair and contains four pigments – black, brown, yellow and red. Finally, the medulla, which is the innermost layer, comprises a core of soft keratin cells.

HAIR LOSS

According to leading hair experts, the amount of hair that you have is relative to your hair colour. Apparently, those with blonde hair have 140,000 hairs on their heads; redheads have 110,000; and brunettes have 60,000. It's normal to lose up to 80 hairs a day through washing or combing. Excessive hair loss or thinning, known as alopecia, is becoming more and more widespread, especially in young women. Hair loss can be hereditary; it may be caused by physical stress, such as wearing your hair in over-tight ponytails; it may be caused by local bacterial, viral or fungus infections; or it may be the result of illness, such as scarlet fever and pneumonia, or of drugs, such as antibiotics and cortisone. In addition, environmental and emotional stress causing tension in the scalp can lead to abnormal hair loss, although trichologists, who are experts in hair and scalp problems, believe that relaxation techniques and scalp massage can treat these problems successfully.

Women are particularly prone to hair loss resulting from hormonal changes. Pregnancy, the Pill and the menopause all throw the body's hormone balance into chaos and can lead to moderate or even severe hair loss. Hair reflects physical changes in the body, especially during menstruation and pregnancy. Before a period, hair can become strangely hostile to styling, but with the increase in oestrogen during pregnancy it can take on a new lease of life, appearing thicker and glossier than ever. After pregnancy, when oestrogen levels fall, distressing hair loss is a common problem, as it is when women stop taking the Pill.

There is little that can be done for this sort of hair loss and, as it is usually only temporary, patience is the only answer. You can expect to lose as many as 200 hairs every day, but if hair begins to

fall out in clumps, seek medical advice. Poor diet, anaemia and illness can also cause hair loss, along with over-use of chemical treatments. Vitamin therapy has proved beneficial in many cases of poor hair health, the B complex vitamins and amino acids being the most important.

Healthy hair depends on a healthy diet. No amount of hair preparations, colour, perming or styling aids can transform hair that has been starved of essential nutrients. As hair is the least important of all the human organs, it is not surprising that it gets its supplies from blood that has already been used to feed the major organs like the heart, lungs, liver and kidneys. Nutritional deficiencies are all too often revealed in thin, limp, out-of-condition hair, which lacks vital shine, body and bounce.

HAIR CARE

Most trichologists agree that the frequency of washing hair is unimportant, provided that a mild preparation is used. Frequent washing is essential if you live in a city, where dirt and dust are attracted to the sebum in the scalp. The general consensus is that in order to maintain a head of healthy hair, you need to protect its pH factor or acid mantle. Most hair has a pH of 4.6, while the roots are 2.6 and the scalp is 5.6; the acid scale ranges from 0–7, so hair is very acidic.

Most shampoos are alkaline-based with a pH of around 8 (the alkaline range is from 7–14) and therefore strip away the hair's natural acidity when it is washed. This can cause problems for those with long hair, as it tends to leave hair tangled and dehydrated. To compensate, many hair experts suggest that you use an acidic rinse, such as vinegar or lemon juice, which helps to restore the natural pH, leaving the hair, scalp and roots much more manageable.

When you shampoo your hair, it is best to tip your head upside down over the bath, shower or sink. After rinsing the hair with warm water, apply a small amount of shampoo to your palms and gently massage it through the hair and into the scalp. Rinse with warm water and then apply another small amount of shampoo, concentrating the massage on the scalp. If you can bear it, give your hair a final rinse with cool water, which helps not only to rinse away any superfluous shampoo but also to tone the scalp.

SCALP CARE

The most important consideration in hair care is to look after the scalp. An oily scalp is the result of over-active sebaceous glands, which lead to lank hair. For an oily scalp, pre-wash with the juice of half a lemon or a tablespoonful of vinegar, both diluted in 600 ml (1 pint) of water. Leave on hair for a few minutes, then wash with mild shampoo. A dry scalp results in dry hair. Use a mild shampoo and a pre-wash treatment of almond or jojoba oil to encourage shine and prevent dehydration. If the scalp shows signs of dandruff, treat with care. Dry hair with oily roots is the most difficult combination to treat, and scalp and ends should be cared for separately.

Afro hair also needs special attention. Treat dry scalp and hair with moisturising oils, such as jojoba, peach kernel or olive oil, before washing with a mild shampoo, then follow with a deep conditioner. For Afro hair with oily roots, use a gentle astringent or regulating product on the scalp before washing, then use a mild shampoo and a

NUTRITION FOR HEALTHY HAIR

A well-balanced diet should provide sufficient nutrients, including protein, vitamins and minerals, for healthy scalp and hair.

PROTEIN
Composed of carbon, oxygen, nitrogen, hydrogen and minerals, protein is a combination of small molecules called amino acids – which are, basically, the building blocks of the body.

SOURCES
Meat, fish, poultry, milk, eggs, cheese, yoghurt, sunflower seeds, brewer's yeast.

NUCLEIC ACIDS
Also found in protein, DNA (deoxyribonucleic acid) and RNA (ribonucleic acid) are the body's most important components, carrying our cellular blueprints and genetic information.

SOURCES
Found in fish, liver, beets and vegetables.

VITAMIN A
This is essential for healthy hair. Excessive amounts of Vitamin A can be poisonous (the recommended daily amount is 10,000 mg). It is better to incorporate vitamin A-rich foods into your diet than to take vitamin supplements.

SOURCES
Butter, eggs, milk, carrots, tomatoes, oily fish such as herring, sardines and mackerel, dark green leafy vegetables, yellow vegetables, tomatoes, apricots, cantaloupe.

VITAMIN B
B complex vitamins are essential for optimum health and are particularly beneficial to hair and skin.

SOURCES
Milk, eggs, wholegrain cereals and breads, brewer's yeast, wheatgerm, nuts, soya beans, poultry, fish, meat.

VITAMIN D
Synthesised by the sun, vitamin D is necessary to the absorption of calcium and phosphorus, both of which are essential for healthy hair, teeth and bones.

SOURCES
Sunlight, fish liver oils and oily fish, milk, eggs.

VITAMIN C
Necessary for maintaining a healthy immune system, it helps to strengthen the body's cells and blood vessels.

SOURCES
Blackcurrants, horseradish, green peppers, citrus fruits, bananas, avocados, artichokes, dark green leafy vegetables.

VITAMIN E
Known as the anti-ageing vitamin, it helps to prevent the formation of free radicals in the body.

SOURCES
Wheatgerm, peanuts, vegetable oils, pulses, green leafy vegetables.

IRON
Iron is used by the bone marrow in the body to make new haemoglobin for new red blood corpuscles.

SOURCES
Spinach, cockles, winkles, liver, kidneys, parsley, pulses, lentils, beans, peas, dried fruit.

CALCIUM
This is constantly needed by the body in order to carry out rebuilding work on bones and teeth. It is also necessary for blood clotting and for properly functioning muscles and nervous system.

SOURCES
Cheese, nuts, eggs, milk, yoghurt, sardines, kelp, root vegetables.

IODINE
This is essential for healthy metabolism – the chemical process that produces energy from food. It is also an essential ingredient of the thyroid hormone, thyroxine, and is closely linked to hair growth.

SOURCES
Seafood, dried kelp, iodised salt.

SULPHUR
Sulphur is essential for hair growth.

SOURCES
Many protein foods, such as eggs, meat, cheese, dairy produce.

Protect hair from the elements. Slick on protective gels to guard hair from the drying effect of sun, sea and wind.

deep-conditioning treatment on the hair but not on the scalp.

The most common problem needing treatment is dandruff. If you suffer from dry skin on your body or face, you will most probably have a dry scalp. You can treat this by massaging a light oil, such as jojoba or peach kernel, into the scalp before washing the hair. Dandruff has many forms, however, a few of them not so easy to cure. A flaky scalp coupled with excess oiliness can be a sign of a bacterial scalp infection. The causes are thought to be stress, nervous tension and hormonal imbalance, all of which may need medical attention.

Treat the scalp with a mild anti-dandruff shampoo and ensure that combs and brushes are kept clean. If the scalp seems to be continually dry and flaking, it could be a sign of psoriasis, which should be treated by a dermatologist.

HAIR REPAIR

Although you can nourish hair from within, it is impossible to feed it externally. Conditioners simply repair the hair by clinging to the outside of the hair shaft, rather like polish or varnish, to bring back shine and revitalise condition.

Afro hair is the most difficult to condition, as

PROTECTION FROM THE ELEMENTS

Your skin is not the only thing that can be damaged by the sun; hair suffers, too. Expose unprotected locks to strong sunlight, sea water, chlorine and wind at your peril, for your hair will become discoloured and structurally damaged, leaving it dry and dull. Chemically treated hair is especially vulnerable, as its weakened structure is sensitive to sunlight and the harsh chemicals found in swimming pools.

Protect your crowning glory from the damaging effects of the sun. Holidays in the sun can play havoc with your hair. Heat and sea salt dry out the natural oils, coating the cuticle (the outer layer of each strand) so that microscopic scales become brittle and tend to lift and separate. This allows the loss of water-binding substances and pigment molecules from the inner cortex. For hair that has been treated with perming solutions and chemical colorants, subjected to overzealous washing with strong shampoos or styled with heated implements, a dose of sun and sea can be the final insult.

It is therefore important to take cover with one of the many protective gels and lotions available. These contain sun filters and conditioners that coat each individual hair shaft, protecting against sun damage and keeping the hair in good condition. Apply them before going into the sun and use to slick hair into place.

Give hair a glossy sheen by treating it to a rich remoisturising treatment after a day in the sun. Gently wash the salt out of your hair with a mild shampoo specially formulated for frequent washing, or a shampoo that treats damaged hair. There are special shampoos available that are created specifically to deal with the drying effects of sun, sea and chlorine. When hair is clean, restore it with a rich conditioner. Apply generously to hair, paying particular attention to the ends, which are prone to splitting. Wrap your hair up in a towel for at least 30 minutes to allow for deep-down conditioning. Rinse hair thoroughly, comb through with a wide-toothed comb and dry naturally, away from harsh sunlight.

While there's little to be done for permanently damaged hair, deep-conditioning treatments can often help recovery. They saturate the hair with moisturisers, which are absorbed into the cuticle layer. They then coat it with waxes and oils to

the tight curls prevent an even coating of conditioner. To make it more controllable, Afro hair can be chemically straightened or permed, but this may make it even drier and could damage the scalp.

Hot oils and waxes help to repair hair and to replenish some the lost moisture and oils. Make your own hot oil treatments with almond, jojoba or even olive oil for very dry hair. Pour two tablespoons of your chosen oil into a cup or mug, then place the cup in a bowl of boiling water for two to three minutes to warm the oil gently. Massage the oil into the hair, paying particular attention to the ends – avoid the roots if you have an oily scalp or roots.

smooth down and increase the cohesion of cuticles, which seals in moisture and restores lustre. If your hair is fine, these conditioners may prove too heavy, leaving it lank. Look for formulas that contain cationic (positively charged) polymers, which cling to the hair, especially the damaged parts, adding body and combating static. Conditioners enriched with fragmented or hydrolysed proteins are also excellent. These protein particles infiltrate the cuticle layer, especially if the scales are lifted by heating, and improve the elasticity of hair.

Heat aids conditioning treatments, so apply while bathing, or wrap hair in a warm, damp towel. If necessary, seek professional help.

The nutrients needed to build healthy hair reach the follicles, where the hair grows, through tiny blood vessels. If the head muscles contract, through tension, these vessels are compressed, so impairing the free flow of blood. Regular scalp massage is one of the most effective ways to release muscle tension. After washing hair, work through a tablespoon of almond oil, to which three drops

each of essential oils of lavender, juniper, rosemary and cypress have been added. This will help to condition the scalp and stimulate healthy hair growth. Leave on for 30 minutes, then wash away with a mild shampoo.

Winter also takes its toll on hair. Central heating, low humidity and too much heat styling are the main villains. Combating static is a constant problem in winter, as anyone with fine or chemically-treated hair is no doubt already aware. When an electric charge builds up along individual strands of hair it can actually stand on end. Hair care experts have grappled with this problem and have come up with solutions. Friction is the primary cause of static and hair can become charged up whenever it is brushed, combed or even stroked. Synthetic materials create more of a charge than natural fibres, so if static is a real problem, it is well worth investing in a wooden comb and natural bristle brush. Longer-lasting benefits come from the regular use of conditioners. These work to combat static in two ways: first, they should con-

From long to short and snappy, a precision haircut offers an easy to manage option for those on the run.

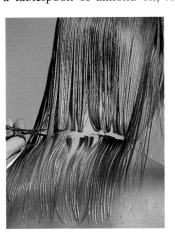

tain positively charged ingredients, which cancel out the negative charge; and second, they coat the hair with special lightweight emollients to guard against friction.

Static is less of a problem in the summer months because of higher humidity. In winter, spray water into the air after drying your hair or invest in a humidifier for your office or home.

Hair colour tends to look duller in winter time, as the subtle lights given by the sun fade. As a result, we are more likely to have it coloured. But if your hair is already difficult to control, permanent tints can make matters worse. Instead, go for wash-in, semi-permanent tints, which also condition hair. Traditionalists may prefer the very subtle effects of natural rinses, based on chamomile for blondes and rosemary for brunettes.

MODERN HAIRSTYLES

When you choose a hairstyle, think carefully about your lifestyle. How much time do you have in the morning before you go to work? How much effort and expense will it take to maintain the style? Will it fit in with the clothes that you wear or with your job? A good hairdresser should also consider all of these points before cutting, colouring or perming your hair and should first discuss them with you.

Modern hairstyles should be easy to maintain and versatile. Experiment with hair accessories to dress hair up for glamorous evenings, summer holidays and special occasions. Look out for unusual clips, pins, scarves and hairbands, which can transform hair in a matter of minutes. Avoid anything that is going to take hours to arrange, unless you know you've got plenty of time to spare.

No matter what style you choose, a professional cut is essential.

STYLING PRODUCTS

Knowing what styling products to use to maintain your style and how to use them correctly is also very important. Mousse, gel, fixing spray, pomade, oil and hairspray all have different styling properties (see chart opposite). Most styling products contain polymers, which help to create an invisible film on each hair, so protecting it from humidity and helping to retain the hair style. Polymers also create an illusion of body and volume, as they coat and thicken each strand.

Modern hairstyles reflect the new freedom of fashion. Long, straight hair can be dressed with hair oil to give a healthy shine. Apply an old-fashioned brilliantine to a modern 90s crop to create shine and movement.

PROPERTIES OF HAIR-STYLING PREPARATIONS

GEL

Gel contains water, alcohol and polymers. It can be used on dry hair to give hold and shine, or on wet hair to create a slick polished finish. It is for firm-hold styles, which are ideal for summer and the beach.

SERUM

Serums contain silicone which coats the hair shaft. This makes hair appear thicker, while creating a glossy shine. Use a few drops on frizzy, coarse or dull hair before styling to detangle and smooth out the hair cuticle and after blow-drying to boost shine.

MOUSSE

Alcohol or water-based, an opaque foam which coats each hair, so improving hair volume and body. It is ideal to add body to fine hair and to set hair on rollers or when blow-drying.

POMADE

A solid oil-based wax can be used to add gloss to short hair, or to give shine to the ends of long hair.

BRILLIANTINE

An oil-based cream which makes hair smooth and shiny, it is traditionally used by men but now also by women with short hair. Use it to slick hair back or massage a little into curly hair to revive curl and restore lustre.

SETTING LOTION

A lotion containing alcohol, water and polymers, it coats the hair and protects it. Apply to hair before setting on rollers, blow-drying and finger-waving.

STYLING SPRAY

This has a combination of the properties of gel, setting lotion and hairspray, and can be used to style hair or to give it a light hold. Ideal for short hair and to set hair that has been curled.

HAIRSPRAY

Available in many different guises and strengths, hairsprays generally contain water, polymers and sometimes alcohol. Designed to coat the hair with an invisible mist, which gives hold to all lengths of hair.

PERMANENT WAVING

To perm hair, it is necessary to break the chemical bonds that hold the protein molecules together. Hairdressers use various chemical lotions, which are usually highly alkaline, to dissolve the bonds. The alkalinity of the lotion swells and softens the hair shaft, so allowing the bond-breaking chemicals to penetrate. There are three main types of perm available – conventional, acid and soft-wave. A conventional perm uses ammonium thioglycolate to break the bonds; an acid perm contains glycol monothioglycolate and, because it uses a pH of between 6 and 7, it causes less damage to the hair and produces a softer curl; soft-wave perms, which use bisulfites to break the bonds, are weaker than conventional perming chemicals, are most often used in home-perming products and only last for about six to eight weeks.

When you decide to have a perm, always seek the advice of a professional hairdresser. Ensure that he or she examines the condition of your hair carefully and that you explain exactly what chemical treatments you have used on your hair in the last year.

Before you have your hair permed, you or your hairdresser should consider five important factors: porosity; thickness of hair; elasticity; volume; and length. The porosity of the hair is its ability to absorb liquid. You need to know this in order to work out how long the perming solution should be left on. The more porous the hair, the less time the perm should need. Hair that has been coloured is much more porous than virgin hair and so should be treated with extra care. Hairdressers should always test a few strands of hair with perming lotion before they perm the whole head. Hair thickness also determines how quickly the perming solution will take to be absorbed – fine hair will obviously absorb the perm more quickly than coarse hair. The hair's natural elasticity depends on moisture content. Sun-damaged, coloured and badly-treated hair that is lacking moisture can become brittle, which can affect how well it holds curl or wave. The natural volume of

hair also reflects what sort of result will be achieved. Full hair demands larger rollers, while thin, sparse hair should be permed on smaller rollers. Hair length also has to be considered. Most modern perms are designed for all lengths of hair but the skill of the hairdresser is of paramount importance in the success of the perm on longer lengths of hair. The rollers must be wound with an even tension in order to achieve the same effect from the roots to the ends.

HAIR COLOURING

Careful use of hair colorants can brighten and enliven hair and can even improve the condition. There are several varieties of permanent hair colorant – aniline, vegetable and metallic. Aniline dyes oxidise on the hair to create the desired colour; vegetable dyes (see chart, right) coat the hair and dye the shaft; and metallic dyes are used to colour grey hair by depositing a coat of dye on the surface. Temporary and semi-permanent colours are used as rinses, enhancing colour for up to six shampoos.

VEGETABLE DYES

Dyes that are made from vegetable extracts usually give great shine and warmth to the hair. Used with care, they can create brilliant effects – but always err on the side of caution, as it is better to use a little at first and to build up colour intensity than to use too much and be stuck with permanent results.

HENNA
Perfect for adding warmth to black, chestnut and auburn hair, henna is derived from the leaves of the Lawsonia plant. It stains the outer cuticle of the hair and does not penetrate into the hair shaft. Never use henna if you have used a metallic-based hair dye, or if you want to have your hair permed. Henna gives a permanent colour, although it does gradually fade. Seek out pure henna powders – some may be combined with metallic substances and these are best avoided. Egyptian and Persian hennas are usually the best quality. You can add coffee, red wine or sage to achieve different effects. Mix up the henna powder with warm water to make a paste. Add an egg and a teaspoon of olive oil to the paste for essential conditioning. It is best to test the colour on a few strands of hair before you colour all of your hair. For the best results, leave henna on for 30–40 minutes.

RHUBARB ROOT
A potent hair brightener, rhubarb roots add chestnut highlights to black hair and golden tones to ash blonde hair. The effects are permanent. To colour hair, combine 50 g (2 oz) of rhubarb root with 600 ml (1 pint) of white wine and simmer in a covered pan for 20–30 minutes. Leave to cool, then add 1½ tsp of kaolin powder to the strained liquid to make a paste. Apply to hair and leave on for 30 minutes.

CHAMOMILE
Best used on naturally blonde hair, chamomile brightens and highlights fair hair. Again, the results are permanent although the colour may fade, and it is best used as a lightening rinse. Make an infusion with three tablespoons of chamomile flowers in 400 ml (14 fl oz) of boiling water, adding a teaspoon of vinegar and four tablespoons of lemon juice. Leave to cool, then pour over freshly washed hair and leave on for 30 minutes.

MARIGOLD
Adding golden tones to fair hair, marigold colours hair permanently. Make an infusion, as above, using four tablespoons of marigold flowers. Pour over freshly washed hair and leave on for 15 to 20 minutes. Rinse out with warm water.

SAGE
An excellent enricher for dark hair, sage can be mixed with tea to add deep mahogany tones. The results are temporary. Make an infusion as above, using four tablespoons of red sage. Pour over freshly washed hair and leave on for 20 minutes. Rinse thoroughly with warm water.

WALNUTS
Ideal for dark hair, walnuts give a rich, semi-permanent colour that can be used as an enlivening rinse. Make an infusion with two or three handfuls of dried walnuts.

Add brightness and life to every hair colour with careful use of hair colorants and natural vegetable dyes.

CHAPTER SEVEN

MODERN BEAUTY

Modern beauty is all about individuality, freedom from rules and regulations, and enhancing your best features. Groomed and grown-up, the face of modern beauty is created with a clever, sophisticated combination of hi-tech cosmetics. The way in which make-up is being used nowadays is changing not only the way we look, but also how we feel about ourselves. Make-up should always be a reflection of you – your spirit, mood and personality. You can experiment with colour, play with textures, paint with light and shade, and create a look that suits the moment. From natural neutrals to brilliant brights, colour can be used to achieve a new, fresh look. Bring out the best in yourself and learn how to create an up-to-date make-up look that will last from dawn until dusk. Follow expert advice on make-up application, which is just as important as the products you use. Get ready, get set, go! The no-nonsense 10-minute make-up is the perfect fast face for women on the move. ELLE shows you how to create a brave new face.

SECOND SKIN
A GUIDE TO PERFECT MAKE-UP

ELLE beauty has always emphasised the value of enhancing your natural assets, rather than trying to change or camouflage them. This modern philosophy abandons the outdated idea of striving for classical perfection.

Modern make-up is no longer geared to fashion and colour trends, but rather to enhancing the individual. No longer do you need a multitude of cosmetics to create your look – a handful is sufficient to take you through from morning until night. Hi-tech, versatile and long-lasting, modern cosmetics make life a whole lot easier for the busy woman who has little time to spare.

Forget the old preconceptions of beauty. Modern beauty is decidedly natural rather than contrived. It is sexy, sensual, even sensational – but it is also subtle. It's not the obvious lipgloss, scarlet pout, false eyelashes and fake beauty mark any more. Modern beauty gives women boundless freedom to be themselves. There is no one make-up look or stereotype that is representative of modern beauty.

In essence, today's face encompasses the qualities of vitality, sensuality, imperfection and individuality. No longer do we have to hide behind our make-up or camouflage our own natural radiance. Features should be emphasised rather than overpowered. The spirit is both sophisticated and expressive. Pick out your best asset – it might be a strong eyebrow, a dark, smoky eye or a full, accentuated mouth – and flaunt it by emphasising, enhancing and dramatising. Don't be tempted to draw attention to all your features at once – your face will end up looking unbalanced and over made-up.

No longer is colour used for the sake of it. It has to be right for your skin tone. The new 'no make-up' make-up achieves what every woman wants: a sheer protective veil which guards her skin from the environment, a healthy, natural-looking complexion, accentuated features and a radiant glow.

PRIMED FOR ACTION

A perfect base demands careful application and tailor-made products that complement your natural skin tone. Start from scratch and prepare skin with corrective primers and concealers. A smooth, even finish depends on a perfectly primed skin. In winter, when all complexions can look dull and lacklustre, or in the evening when skin is tired, apply a skin-priming fluid. Designed to illuminate skin and to conceal shadows, primers work by increasing the amount of light reflected from the skin's surface and also prepare the skin for foundation and powder by providing a smooth, even base. Dot the primer on under the eyes and on the chin, forehead, cheeks and chin, and blend prior to applying your foundation.

You can also use colour-corrective primers to neutralise a red complexion, add life to a sallow skin or brighten up a dull face. Alleviate redness by applying a green primer. Use only the smallest amount of primer, blending it with a little moisturiser before applying it. Dot it on to any reddened areas and blend carefully. For sallow skin, pale pink or lilac primers work wonders. Again dilute with moisturiser, dot on to sallow areas and blend to achieve the best results. And dull, tired skin can benefit from a touch of white or ivory. Dot on under the eyes, across the cheekbones, under the chin and across the eyelids to enliven and illuminate lacklustre skin.

TOUCH BASE

Ultimately, a clear, radiant complexion is the most important beauty prerequisite. Modern foundations and powders can help to protect skin from the elements and from environmental hazards, acting like a second skin. Versatile, easy to apply and long-lasting, cosmetic technology has enabled us to create the perfect canvas for make-up. Available to suit every skin texture, condition and colour, the latest foundations and powders can correct, camouflage, enhance, protect, moisturise, and even minimise sebum production. With help like this anyone can create a beautiful complexion.

For those with an even skin tone, touch up blemishes, shadows and skin tone irregularities with a little foundation and dust the face with some loose powder. This light-handed approach can work just as well for blemished skin. It is preferable to use a minimal make-up base than to apply heavy foundation. Use base where and when you need it and, if possible, have your base custom-blended to match your skin tone exactly, so as to allow the natural colour of skin to shine through. Using a damp sponge to blend the foundation, dot it under the eyes, around the nose, and to even out skin tone.

ELLE'S TOP MAKE-UP ARTISTS TIPS FOR PERFECT MODERN MAKE-UP

TIPS FOR A BETTER BASE

LUCIA PIERONI
'Use a foundation with a built-in moisturiser or mix your own foundation with a few drops of moisturiser to achieve a smooth even finish. Use a sponge to apply foundation under the eyes – just dab it on gently and then use your fingertips to blend it in. A water spray is an excellent investment – spray it on to your skin before applying foundation – it helps to close the pores and creates a matt finish. Always choose a loose, fine-textured powder to dust over your foundation to protect and preserve the base.'

LESLEY CHILKES
'The most important feature of your make-up has to be your base. One foolproof tip is to mix moisturiser with foundation or concealers before applying it to the skin. This gives an even tone and prevents streaking.'

CAROL BROWN
'Custom-blended foundation and powders ensure that you can create the perfect base and match it exactly to your own skin tone. Apply foundation lightly. You can always apply a second layer if you need to. When buying foundations, loose or compact powder, always ask for a sample and test the colour in natural daylight. The light in department stores can be deceptive, so it's often difficult to tell what matches your skin tone.'

FRANCES HATHAWAY
'For a more natural look, use a concealer to even out skin tone and cover up blemishes. Mix it with a little moisturiser before you apply it. Then dust the face with loose powder to create a matt finish.'

CLEVER CONCEALING

The next step is to conceal any blemishes, imperfections or shadows with a liquid or cream concealer. Paint on concealer with a fine make-up brush for precision and easy blending. For a more natural day look, use a few drop of moisturiser to dilute the concealer for sheerer coverage.

Alternatively, if you need more coverage, you can apply your foundation after you conceal imperfections. Blend the concealer carefully with your index finger using light, dabbing movements. Pat on a little loose powder to keep make-up fresh.

COLOUR CODES

From the palest creamy complexion to the darkest mahogany, skin deserves foundation and powder that are matched as closely as possible to its natural colouring. Look out for custom-blended foundations that are individually prepared to match your skin tone. Skin has its own natural undertones and everyone's skin is made up of several different colour nuances.

When you're choosing a foundation to suit your skin tone, select three or four shades that are closest to your skin colour and dot them on to your jawline, ensuring it has been cleansed of any previous traces of make-up. The shade best suited to your skin will blend almost imperceptibly.

POWDER PERFECTION

The advances in modern cosmetic engineering have made what was once thought impossible a reality. The latest space-age powders are made from micro-fine particles and microscopic bubbles, so small and light that they are barely perceptible.

Not only do they help to fix foundation, but they double as skin treatments, helping to protect, moisturise, and maintain an even texture. The technology of micro-encapsulation has enabled scientists to create multi-purpose, featherweight, translucent powders, which also incorporate active treatment ingredients in the same formula, so ensuring that your skin is protected from the harmful effects of environmental hazards.

'When applying powder, always use a large soft brush,' advises make-up artist Chase Aston. 'Use small circular movements to dust the powder on as if you were buffing the skin and always work downwards, from the forehead to the chin.'

TYPES OF FOUNDATION

LIQUID FOUNDATIONS

Although there is a wide variety of fluid foundations, the majority give light, sheer coverage. Best suited to combination or oily skin types, which need little additional oil or moisture, they are available in a number of formulations – oil-free; matt; and oil-in-water. Liquid foundations are versatile, too, as you can blend them with a little water to create an extra-sheer base.

COMPACT FOUNDATIONS

Doubling up as powder and foundation, compact bases are extremely versatile and easy to use. Again, there is a variety of formulations: some have a similar texture to that of pressed powder and can be applied with a dry or damp sponge to create a light, natural finish; while others are creamier and provide heavier coverage.

MOUSSE FOUNDATIONS

Using the technology of hair mousses, mousse foundations have the benefit of being light and airy, and are easy both to apply and to blend. Ideal for sheerer coverage on younger skins.

CREAM FOUNDATIONS

Richer in moisturising ingredients than liquid formulations, cream bases give extra coverage and are more suited to dry skins. They also give a slightly dewy finish for those who dislike the matt look.

TINTED MOISTURISERS

With the combined benefits of a moisturiser and a sheer, liquid foundation, tinted moisturisers are the perfect alternative to heavier bases for summer and for young skins that need little coverage.

TINTED AND BRONZING GELS

Offering transparent coverage and a healthy glow, these are ideal for oilier skin and for young skins that need only a hint of cover. Use them to enhance a tan or to add a glow to pallid skins.

THE BEST EYES

The eyes are an important feature of any make-up, whether you choose a natural or glamorous look.

Always ensure that your eyebrows and lashes are well groomed. Shaped and groomed brows are an essential, framing the face and adding strength and definition. Don't just pluck brows at random. Treat yourself to a professional eyebrow shape, which may be more painful but gives you the best results in the long run.

Emphasise brows with a pencil or shadow in a shade that matches your natural hair colouring. Use the pencil to draw light, upward strokes, working from the inner to the outer brow. Use an eyebrow or lash comb or brush to sweep the brows upwards and outwards. Apply a little Vaseline to the brows to add shine in the evening.

Lashes should be enhanced with mascara. Brush on a layer of mascara to the upper lashes

10-MINUTE MAKE-UP

The best news about modern make-up is that you don't need hours to apply it. In fact you can create the perfect face in as little as 10 minutes. All you need is a well-stocked kit of high performance essentials and a few fresh ideas.

THE PERFECT BASE

3 minutes

Create a fast finish with the latest foundations, quick to apply and designed to flatter skin tone and to give light, even coverage. Choose from compound foundations, which also double as face powders, tinted moisturisers, airy foundation mousses for the lightest coverage, or filmy fluid bases.

1. Ensure that skin has been thoroughly cleansed and lightly moisturised before applying your base.

2. For a translucent effect, try a tinted moisturiser or fluid foundation, which lets your natural skin tone shine through but helps even out skin colours. Use a damp natural sea sponge and apply the base with smooth strokes evenly over the skin. Blend with fingertips around the eyes and nose. If you are using a compact foundation, dampen the sponge and apply with light sweeping movements, blending to the jawline. The effect should be almost transparent, although you can conceal small blemishes by adding a little extra base where it's needed most.

3. A useful tip to keep your base fresh throughout the day is to spray with a facial mist.

4. Dust the face with a sprinkling of loose powder, using a large soft brush in downward strokes.

FAST EYE DEFINER

4 minutes

The modern make-up look makes the most of minimalism. For quickly defined eyes, forget complicated blends of different colours and stick to simple shading and lighting techniques. Go for matt shadows or cream ones with a slight luminosity, but avoid glittery shadows at all costs. Not only do they take hours to apply properly, but they tend to be messy and are difficult to blend.

1. Choose shading and highlighting colour – for example, taupe to shade the eye and beige to highlight the lid or brow. Stick to skin-flattering tones, such as taupe, mushroom, grey and apricot.

2. With a small brush or sponge applicator, shade lids with the darker colour. Blend it into the crease of the eye and follow the eye's natural contours.

3. To give extra definition, sweep a little highlighter across the brows with a soft eyeshadow brush and smooth away any hard lines created by the darker shade.

4. Lightly brush on a complementary mascara.

5. After defining the lashes, shape eyebrows with a brush, using short upward and outward strokes.

A RADIANT GLOW

1 minute

Lightly dip a large blusher brush into a rosy powder blush and then into a little loose powder and dust on to the 'apples' of the cheeks. Add just enough colour to give a hint of blush and don't be tempted to paint stripes of colour along the cheekbones. The effect should be soft and subtle.

2. Lightly sweep away excess with a clean cotton-wool ball.

3. For those with dark skin or a tan, try using amber or terracotta shades dusted on in the same way. Sweep the colour across the temples, under the chin and over the eyelids for a healthy glow.

LIP SERVICE

2 minutes

Creating the perfect pout has never been easier than it is now with the new array of quick-draw lip pens, brushes and sponge-tipped glosses.

1. Apply a lip balm to soften the lips. A tip for soft lips is to brush them gently with a soft clean toothbrush to which you apply a dot of lip balm. Tissue off excess balm and apply the first coat of colour. Blot with a tissue and then outline and colour lips with a lip pencil. Blend with a lip brush and blot with a tissue for a stained effect.

2. For summer or when playing sports, dab a little lip gloss on to the centre of the lower lip to accentuate lips and enhance fullness.

10 SPEEDY HINTS

● Keep your make-up essentials together, ensuring that brushes and sponges are always clean and dry. A tip to keep sponges and brushes extra-clean is to soak them in a weak solution of sterilising fluid, such as Milton. Rinse them thoroughly with cold, clean water.

● Don't experiment with new colours when you are in a hurry. Stick to those that flatter and enhance skin, eyes and hair colouring.

● For a quick day-to-night make-up change, keep an eyeliner pen on hand for fast glamour. Use it to line the upper lid thinly.

● Look out for products that double up: colourless mascaras that can be used to shape lashes and brows: clever compact lip powders that double as eyeshadows or blushers.

● Choose matt blushers and eyeshadows rather than glittery ones, as they are easier to use and more flattering.

● Look for eyeshadow duos that combine a shader and highlighter.

● Always use a damp sponge to apply your foundation. It gives a sheerer and more natural finish. You can use your fingers to blend.

● Use a cream concealer to hide blemishes after you've applied your base. It's easier to blend and will conceal any imperfections more effectively.

● Apply your make-up in a well-lit place, preferably by a window.

● Use just a little make-up. Remember that less is better – you can always add another coat or intensify the colour later for evening drama.

THE PERFECT MAKE-UP FOR FOUR SKIN COLOURINGS

THE PERFECT FRECKLED COMPLEXION

1. Use a light fluid concealer to mask shadows and blemishes. It's better to have a light, natural base than to try to hide freckles under a heavy base.

2. Blend white primer with light beige foundation to make a concealer. Dot lightly around the eyes and cover any imperfections. Blend without dragging the skin around the eyes.

3. Freckled skin needs only a little powder. Dust off with a small powder brush.

4. Enhance and emphasise. As freckles tend to dominate the face, draw attention to the eyes by lining them with a soft, smudgy pencil.

5. Smudge the soft pencil close to the lashes. Choose muted browns and soft greys for a natural look, rather than black which can look too harsh against paler skin tones.

6. Brush on dark brown mascara and separate the lashes with a soft bristle eyebrow brush. Shape the eyebrows with a fine brush, combing them through with matt brown shadow.

7. For a natural finish, apply a rosy-coloured lip gloss, mixing it with rosewater to keep lips soft. Dab on the colour with a cotton bud for a stained look. Dust on some rust-coloured blusher to add a glow to cheeks.

THE PERFECT FAIR COMPLEXION

1. Fair skin shows up blemishes more easily than darker skin, so match up a light concealer and foundation.

2. To help disguise blemishes, dark shadows and uneven skin tones, stroke on a concealing cream under the eyes, and around the nose and chin, blending it carefully without dragging the delicate skin around the eyes.

3. In addition to concealer, try using a colour-correcting primer if the skin has any red patches or tends to blush easily. Smooth it on to the appropriate areas and blend with a sponge.

4. Dot foundation on to the cheeks, chin and forehead. Blend and dust with translucent powder.

5. Colour eyes with matt brown shadow, dust cheeks with a soft bronze blusher and stain lips with a berry red gloss blended with lip balm.

THE PERFECT DARK COMPLEXION

1. Most dark skins have uneven patches of colour, which need to be evened out and blended in to match the rest of the complexion.

2. Apply a concealer two shades lighter than your natural colouring to areas where pigmentation is darker or uneven.

3. Apply a fluid, oil-free foundation in a shade lighter than your skin colour. Alternatively, have a custom-blended foundation made to match your own skin tone.

4. Powder lightly with a translucent powder. For very dark or black skin, you may need to use a tinted powder instead.

5. Dust lilac or pink powder lightly across the skin to add warmth. Apply a matt blusher in russet or bronze.

6. Colour eyes with grey or deep violet eyeshadow and stain lips with a rich raspberry shade to match natural lip tone.

THE PERFECT OLIVE COMPLEXION

1. Olive skin can often appear sallow, so foundations with pink undertones can be uplifting. Cover any blemishes or shadows with concealer, blending it carefully.

2. Use a damp sponge to blend foundation. Smooth it over the skin, remembering to cover the ears and to blend it carefully into the jawline.

3. Dust on a lilac-coloured corrective powder. Use a large, soft brush to apply powder liberally, dusting it all over the face and neck.

4. Brush away any excess corrective powder with a clean, soft brush. For best results, sweep the skin finely with large circular strokes.

5. Shade eyes with dark brown or mauve and give lips a rosy tint. Skin may need a light dusting of powder to 'set' the base.

and then comb through with a lash comb or brush. For evening, apply a second coat and comb through. Alternatively, for a more natural effect, curl lashes with eyelash curlers. Ensure that lashes are clean and free from mascara. Clamp the eyelash curlers on to the lashes, hold for 30 seconds and release. For extra shine and emphasis, apply a little Vaseline to the tips of the lashes with your fingertip, stroking it across lightly.

Modern eye make-up is easy to apply. Whether you choose creamy, crease-resistant shadow, or smooth pressed powders, always use a brush or sponge-tipped applicator to apply and blend the colour.

For the best results, don't use more that two shades on the lids. A rainbow of colours may look seductive in the palette but using a multitude of shades on your eyes is both distracting and old-fashioned. Keep eye make-up simple. Go for a monotone look – use one colour on the lid, blend it from the lashes up to the crease and wing it gently upwards and outwards towards the tip of your eyebrow; or use two complementary shades, a shader and a highlighter, which you can use to contour and emphasise the eyes.

For evening drama, use an eyeliner pen or pencil on the top lid to add a hint of glamour. Make-up artist Ruby Hammer has a foolproof tip for applying liner. 'Always steady your hand by placing your elbow on a hard surface or support your elbow with your other hand. Instead of looking straight ahead into your mirror, use a small hand mirror, which you should place on flat surface – this way you can look down when applying the liner and are less likely to make mistakes or get the liner in your eyes.'

GLOW EASY

The modern way to use blusher adds a healthy, vital glow to paler skin tones, enhances darker complexions and gives sparkle to sun-kissed skins. Forget the old ways of applying blusher – it should be used to add a little colour and warmth to the cheeks, not to sculpt the face. For instance, if you have a round face, enhance it instead of trying to disguise it – the last thing to do is to paint stripes of blusher across your cheeks in the hope that you might sculpt them by creating an optical illusion. Instead, use blusher to enhance your natural skin colouring and to give a healthy vital glow.

To apply blusher, use a large, soft brush. Build up the intensity of colour gradually, rather than applying too much and then having to remove it. Dab it on to the apples of your cheeks, where you blush naturally, and to the places on your face that are illuminated by the sun – forehead, temples and eyelids. In the evening, you can also dust a little blusher under your chin and on to your shoulders and decolleté. In the summer, use a bronzing powder in lieu of foundation. Moisturise skin, pat dry with a tissue and then dust the face with bronzer with a large, soft brush. This creates a healthy, sun-tanned glow.

LIP TIPS

Even if you usually wear no other make-up than a light foundation and a hint of mascara, lipstick can add the perfect finish.

When you apply your foundation, you should always cover the lips to create an even base. Then prime the lips by applying a small amount of soothing and softening lip balm. Dot it on with a fingertip and massage in. If you have rough or chapped lips, use a soft-bristled toothbrush to brush the balm on to the lips. This will help to exfoliate any rough skin and leave lips smooth.

The next step is to apply your lipstick. For day, choose matt or sheer textures, while in the evening, you can opt for richer, creamier lipsticks. Always apply lip colour with a fine brush, using it both to outline and to fill. Load the brush with colour and follow your natural lip contour carefully. Use your other hand to steady your elbow to ensure a perfect result.

Changing and disguising your natural lipline is not easy – it can look messy and may demand constant retouching throughout the day. It's better to enhance your natural lip shape rather than attempting to camouflage it.

Once you've applied your first coat, blot with a single layer of tissue and reapply. You can also use loose powder to set lipstick by dusting it on over the layer of tissue, which acts like a sieve.

Then add a little gloss or balm for glamorous occasions. Keep away from bright, garish colours in the daytime and opt for neutral, muted shades. Strong reds, hot pinks and vibrant oranges work best in the evening or on tanned skins. If you choose a strong lip colour, apply neutral eye colours, such as beige, taupe, grey or black. Never clash lip and eye colours.

TOP TIPS FOR BEST LIPS

LAURIE STARRETT
'Always use a lip brush to apply colour. You'll get a longer-lasting, more professional finish. Avoid using a lipliner that is more than a shade darker than your lipstick. No matter how much you try to blend the two colours, it will always look unnatural.'

MIRANDA JOYCE
'Create a natural-looking lip stain by applying a matt lipstick. Paint on the colour with a lip brush and blot with a tissue. Then reapply for extra intensity.'

RUBY HAMMER
'Rub lips with lipliner or lipstick to stain lips, then add lip balm to soften them. For a matt and long-lasting finish, use lipliner on its own.'

CHASE ASTON
'To prime lips and keep them in perfect condition, apply a little lip balm or Vaseline and brush them gently with a baby-soft toothbrush. For fast, foolproof lips, use your finger or a lipbrush to dot on a little tinted lip gloss and blend. Your lips will look perfectly made-up with very little effort.'

CHAPTER EIGHT

SOLAR POWER

How harmful is sunlight to our skin? Can we really protect ourselves from the harmful effects of ultraviolet light? What sun protection factor will be an adequate sun shield? Like it or not, dermatologists believe that sunlight plays a major role in the process of skin ageing and is responsible for certain types of skin cancer. There is no doubt that sunlight is beneficial to our psychological and physical well-being, and evidence that a lack of sunlight can actually be detrimental to our health is only just coming to light. But research has also clearly highlighted the hazards of tanning. The good news is that you don't have to hide away all summer to avoid harmful ultraviolet rays. You can protect your skin, and tan as safely as is possible, if you use the correct sun protection for your skin type and follow a few golden rules.

SUN WORSHIP
PROTECT TO SURVIVE

The sun has been an object of man's worship for thousands of years. A symbol of life-giving energy, its solar rays are earth's essential life-support system. Yet the sun has become the focus of one of the most controversial scientific debates. To tan or not to tan? Some scientists claim that sun does us the world of good. Others maintain that it is the skin's worst enemy and that it can actually undermine our immune system. But most of us get great pleasure from sunbathing and a golden tan is one of the most potent health tonics. It makes us feel healthy and physically attractive. The last thing that any of us think of when we are lying on a golden beach is skin cancer and wrinkles. Yet suntanning has become a potentially explosive issue, with many experts preaching total abstinence in the name of skin preservation.

Despite the dangers of sunlight to our skin, the latest health research shows that sun does play a positive role in maintaining a healthy body. In fact, sunlight deprivation can be highly detrimental, leading to a condition known as Seasonal Affective Disorder (SAD). According to recent research, sunlight directly influences the body's hormonal balance and, in particular, the hormone melantonin. Melantonin (not to be confused with melanin, the brown pigment that is released when ultraviolet hits our skin to create a tan) has been shown to influence mood, fertility and sleeping patterns, and the amount of sunlight that enters the eye appears to be the all-important switch controlling the production of hormones.

Dr Alfred J Lewy PhD, a research psychiatrist at the National Institute of Mental Health, Maryland, US, explains its effect. 'Melantonin is released from the pineal gland in the brain, normally at night, and has been found to play a vital role in the timing of the body's seasonal rhythms.' Research suggests that lack of sunlight increases the production of melantonin, which results in symptoms of fatigue, depression, certain food cravings, especially for carbohydrates, and general aches and pains.

Melantonin has also been found to suppress the production of insulin by the pancreas, causing a rise in blood sugar. In normal health, the blood sugar is regulated by the body and prevented from going either too high or too low. High blood sugar can lead to cravings and mood swings and scientists believe that sunlight can help to restore the equilibrium of blood sugar levels.

In addition to the effect that sunlight deprivation has on mood, research has also shown that sunlight is an important preventative in the brittle bone disease, osteoporosis. Scientists believe that the elderly are particularly susceptible to osteoporosis in winter, when they spend most of the their time indoors. Because sunlight plays a vital role in the process of calcium absorption in the body, the fewer the hours of sun exposure, the less the absorption of calcium and the greater the risk of osteoporosis. Although there is little that we can do to change the seasons and to brighten the dark winters, scientists have discovered that simulated sunlight, in the form of full-spectrum fluorescent tube lighting, can help to alleviate many of the symptoms of SAD and stabilise the production of melantonin, as well as improving the performance and mood of people who spend most of the daylight hours, regardless of the season, working in artificially lit environments. Tests carried out by doctors in the US and Europe have revealed that full-spectrum lighting can also help decrease the risk of osteoporosis. Although sunlight is almost inextricably linked with the most serious form of skin cancer, malignant melanoma, solar rays are now thought to act as a deterrent against certain forms of breast and colonic cancer. In addition, 25 years ago, Dr John Ott, a researcher at the Environmental Health and Light Research Institute in the US, discovered a link between leukaemia in children and sunlight deprivation. Investigating a very high rate of leukaemia at a school in Illinois, he found that children who spent most of their time in a classroom that had no natural daylight, only warm white fluorescent, were most susceptible to leukaemia. After the lights had been replaced with full-spectrum lighting, there were no further reported cases of the disease at the school.

According to the American Association for the Advancement of Science, the stimulated vitamin D production triggered by sunlight helps to protect us against these forms of cancer. Studies in Russia and the US reveal that the incidence of these cancers is higher in regions where there are low levels of sunshine and, therefore, lower levels of vitamin D. The studies concluded that, although diet was an important factor, the sun was primarily responsible for the lower cancer rates.

Vitamin D, known as the 'Sunshine Vitamin',

is well known to be associated with the calcification of bones. When sunlight strikes the skin, the vitamin is activated and converted into a compound which causes rapid stimulation of calcium absorption by the intestine, which is then incorporated into the bloodstream. The amount of Vitamin D required by an adult is about 20 µg per day, but it can be stored in sufficient amounts in the liver for a single dose to last for some weeks.

According to Dr Cedric Garland, of the University of California, San Diego, solar radiation produces three-quarters of the body's required level of vitamin D. The rest is obtained from food sources, particularly liver and oily fish. As yet, scientists have not been able to pinpoint how vitamin D actually protects against these forms of cancer. Dr Garland believes that vitamin D causes the tissue cells in the breast and colon to bind very tightly when vitamin D is administered. Tightly bound cells grow together in a very regulated way, with individual and possibly precancerous cells being kept in control. He believes that, when vitamin D is absent, the cellular binding loosens, leaving rogue cancer-prone cells to grow uncontrolled, which could, in certain cases, eventually lead to cancer. Researchers also suggest that a diet rich in oily fish, such as herring, or supplemented with cod-liver oil, together with daily sunlight exposure of at least half an hour, could help to protect against breast and colon cancer.

WHAT IS A TAN?

Basically, a tan is the body's natural protective reaction against danger. The danger is, of course, ultraviolet light, and tanning is a mechanism that has been programmed into our skin cells to protect us from these harmful rays. Bearing this in mind, many dermatologists argue that the idea of a 'safe tan' is an anachronism and that, by consciously suntanning or sunbathing, all that we are doing is triggering the skin's in-built alarm system time and time again.

But how do we actually get a tan? When ultraviolet light hits our skin, it triggers off a complex chain of chemical reactions that alter the colour or pigmentation of the skin. The pigment is produced by cells called melanocytes, which produce a dark brown to black pigment called melanin. Sunlight increases the production of melanin, which is really the body's own built-in sunscreen and protects the skin from further damage.

EARLY PROTECTION

While sunlight plays a valuable role in maintaining a balanced and healthy lifestyle, there is now no doubt that careless over-exposure to sun can cause severe skin damage. Not only does it accelerate the ageing process, it can also lead to malignant melanoma. 'All the changes that we think of as ageing – the wrinkling, the blotching, the bumps – aren't ageing at all. It is sun damage,' emphasises Dr Barbara Gilchrest of the Harvard Medical School. Protection has to start young, as scientists now believe that around 70 per cent of skin damage caused by the sun occurs during childhood. Even though the damage may not be seen until much later in life, the havoc wreaked by sun on delicate baby skin can be irreparable. Yet many parents let their children suffer severe sunburn year after year, without any attempt to protect their skin properly.

It is the fairer-skinned Europeans, particularly those of Celtic descent, who are most at risk. If our skin is adequately protected during these early years and never allowed to burn, then, by our 20s, we should have little sun damage. At this age, our skin also possesses a higher degree of natural protection and is therefore more capable of guarding against solar damage.

Recent studies in Australia, which has the highest incidence of melanoma in the world, have

Although a tan is aesthetically pleasing, the internal damage caused to the skin structure is irrefutable.

shown that Europeans who came to the country before the age of 10 have the same risk of developing a melanoma as the native-born Australian. There is a lower risk, however, for Europeans who come to the country after the age of 15. This strongly backs up the theory that over-exposure to the sunk in childhood is of critical importance to the possible later development of skin cancer.

So take the experts' advice and protect babies and children from the sun with specially designed products, specifically for babies and young children, to protect their delicate and vulnerable skin.

THE HAZARDS OF TANNING

No one who cares about their health can afford to ignore the warnings about exposing our skin to excessive amounts of ultraviolet radiation. Environmentalists have warned us that sunlight will become increasingly hazardous if the protective ozone layer that encircles the earth continues to be worn away by pollution in the form of chlorofluorocarbons (CFCs). At present, only UVA and UVB light can penetrate the ozone layer, but the deterioration of this protective invisible veil may eventually allow UVC, potentially the most dangerous form of ultraviolet light, to permeate.

We may not know what effect UVC will have on our fragile skins for at least a decade, but research into UVA and UVB clearly highlight the need for extreme caution. In addition to causing sunburn, speeding up the ageing process of our skin and stimulating certain forms of skin cancer, ultraviolet radiation has even been linked to eye cataracts.

Dr John Hawk, head of the Photobiology Unit of St Thomas's Hospital, London, points out the benefits of sunscreens to protect us from some of the harmful effects of sunlight. 'All UV light has some adverse effect on the skin and exposure to it should be undertaken in moderation, especially by the fair-skinned. However, outdoor activities are enjoyable, health-promoting and to be encouraged, so long as care is taken when UV intensity is high by covering up our skin, or using an appropriate sunscreen.'

Recent studies by doctors revealed that the regular use of low SPF sunscreens can significantly reduce ageing caused by the sun. Previous studies had tested only high SPF products, but their study showed that even low SPF sunscreens, such as those used in many cosmetics and skin care preparations,

can also offer protection against photoageing. Their study concluded that while UVA radiation is unlikely to cause burning, it is responsible for skin ageing and so it is important to choose a sun tanning product that provides broad-spectrum protection – against UVA and UVB to ensure that skin is protected to minimise sun-induced ageing.

However, it is not only UV radiation that is implicated. Infrared, once thought to be fairly innocuous and harmless, may also be responsible for skin damage. Infrared (IR) rays account for 50 per cent of the sun's energy and are the rays which give us the pleasant feeling of warmth when we lie in the sun. However, IR penetrates deep into the dermis, causing the capillaries to dilate and resulting in immediate sunburn. The rise in the skin's temperature also causes damage to the skin by disturbing the balance of hyaluronic acid, which keeps skin hydrated by helping to seal in water. IR also damages the collagen and elastin that keeps skin elastic and firm. The good news is that daily exposure to infrared radiation from the sun is not harmful unless the temperature is in excess of 80°F, but protection from IR is very important in hot climates. While there are a few sunscreens that offer IR protection, most do not shield skin from IR and it may be years before scientists find a safe IR screen that will prevent our skin from overheating when exposed to hot sun. Although research is underway to create a combined UV and IR protector which can be taken orally to protect skin cells internally from the sun's harmful rays, the best we can do at present is to take cover in the shade when our skin begins to feel too hot and to protect from the ultraviolet rays with effective sunscreens.

Cover up when the heat is on and protect delicate areas such as shoulders, back and breasts.

THE AGEING RAYS

A tan may make our skin look healthy, but we can't escape the reality that ultraviolet light, whether from a sunbed or from the natural source, speeds up the rate at which our skin ages. If sun protection is practised early in life, photoaging (ageing caused by sun damage) can be postponed for as long as 20 years, according to an American study of over 200 women between the ages of 25 and 65 with varying degrees of sun damage.

The study was conducted by leading American dermatologist Dr James Leyden, professor of dermatology at the University of Pennsylvania. 'In sun-protected skins, ageing changes may be postponed until around 50 years of age, but in sun-exposed skin, sun damage can be seen on women as young as 20.'

Scientists have now isolated UVA as the ageing ray. Until recently, it was thought to be relatively harmless. Dermatologists were aware that UVA tanned the skin without burning – hence its widespread use in modern sunbeds. The latest research, however, now suggests that it has a detrimental effect on the skin.

It has the longest wavelength in the ultraviolet spectrum, and penetrates deep into the skin's basal layer, where essential cell renewal takes place. Dermatologists believe that it damages the cellular DNA, altering the genetic blueprint. By a series of complex chemical reactions, the supportive collagen and elastin fibres, which hold skin together and keep it firm, smooth and essentially youthful, weaken, leading eventually to the formation of lines, wrinkles and age spots.

According to Dr Brian Diffey, a leading

authority in photobiology – the study of the effect of sunlight on the body – at Dryburn Hospital, Durham, it is essential that we protect our skin from UVA. Dr Diffey is also concerned about the growing use of sunbeds that use UVA to tan skin. He is seeing a marked increase in a condition known as Skin Fragility Syndrome among women who use sunbeds three or four times a week. People suffering from this syndrome develop hypersensitive skin, which bruises and blisters easily.

Scientists are also concerned that we have paid too much attention to protecting ourselves from UVB, the ray associated with burning and skin cancer, and not enough to guarding against UVA. They now suggest that we use sun products that contain an equal balance of UVA and UVB filters to give maximum protection. At present, the Sun Protection Factor on a product refers only to the UVB rays. In the Royal College of Physicians' report, The Sun on Your Skin, the use of a SPF of 6 or more is highly recommended at all times when

sun is exposed to strong sunlight. Even though your tan may deepen, they advise that you still keep to a higher factor, since the tan does not protect you from further UVA damage.

Leading dermatologist Dr Oswald Morton believes that protection from UVA is essential. 'All experts agree on the need for high protection, but sunscreens need to offer both UVA and UVB protection. A person using a UVB sun product with poor UVA screening is exposing themselves to longer-term UVA damage. It would be better to use a lower protection product and stay in the sun for a shorter time to cut down on UVA exposure. However, in an ideal world, people should use sunscreens that provide both UVA and UVB filters.'

THE BURNING RAYS

UVB has a shorter wavelength than UVA and is absorbed by the epidermis, the upper layer of skin. Associated with sunburn, UVB has now been linked with skin cancer. In fact, scientists are in no

Although sun may make us look fit and healthy it is undoubtedly damaging to the structure of the skin.

Ensure that the skin is always protected by applying a waterproof sun product. Reapply when you emerge from the water after drying the skin.

Take to the shade and avoid sun damage with self tans that give the benefits of colour without the hazards of sun bathing.

doubt that UVB is responsible for the cellular changes that lead to skin cancer. Protection is the key to preventing skin cancer, especially in childhood. Dermatologists now know that repeated sunburn in our early years, especially for those with fair skins, is likely to result in skin cancer later in life.

According to the Cancer Research Campaign, there has been a 50 per cent increase over a period of ten years in the number of people developing and dying from malignant melanoma in the UK. Alarmingly, new statistics show that the number of people with malignant melanoma is steadily rising each year. There are several schools of thought as to why skin cancer is increasing so rapidly. Some scientists believe that it is linked to the package holiday boom, which took place in the 1970s, while others fear that the depletion of the ozone layer is responsible. The ozone layer shields us from dangerous levels of ultraviolet radiation, specifically the shortest and most dangerous wavelength UVC. However, there is now concern that it is allowing higher levels of UVB and UVA to penetrate the atmosphere, therefore exposing our skin to more sun damage that ever before.

Skin cancer is most common on the face and hands. In fact, 85 per cent of all skin cancers are found in these areas which are exposed to sunlight day in, day out, throughout our lives. Dermatologists

urge us to take heed of their warnings and to protect face and hands from sun damage by using sunscreens which filter both UVA and UVB rays. Some even suggest that the daily use of a moisturiser containing sunfilters can help to reduce the risk of skin cancer and accelerated ageing.

SUN PROTECTION FACTORS

Despite widespread education on sun safety, many people are still bewildered by sun protection. In particular, Sun Protection Factors, or SPFs, remain a mystery to many sun worshippers. In theory, the SPF marked on a sun product indicates how much longer you can stay in the sun without burning while using protection. In the past, the SPF of a product referred to the protection it afforded against UVB – the ray that causes burning and naturally, it was thought that a high SPF ensured a 'safer' tan. Then researchers discovered that using high SPF products could actually cause the skin more harm. This was because they enabled us to stay in the sun longer without burning but still allowed the ageing UVA rays to penetrate deep into the skin. Many suncreens now contain broad-spectrum ultraviolet filters – that means they protect skin from from both UVA and UVB. When buying sun protection, always choose products which afford broad-spectrum protection.

So how do you know which sun protection

factor is right for your skin? We all have a Natural Protection Time or NPT (see Sun Protection Chart); this is the amount of time that skin can be exposed to sunlight without burning. It does vary according to skin colour, how tanned your skin is and the strength of the sun. For instance, those who have an NPT of 10 minutes should be able to stay out safely for six times longer (one hour) if protected by an SPF of 6. Of course, each individual is different and some very fair or freckled skins may burn after as little as five minutes in the sun. Always err on the side of caution when deciding which SPF you need. It really is better to be safe than sorry as letting your skin burn is the worst thing that you can do.

FAKE OR SELF-TANNING PRODUCTS

Nowadays, the only really 'safe' tan comes from a tube or bottle. Fake or self-tanning creams, gels, sprays and lotions offer a golden glow without exposing skin to the sun at all. They work by 'staining' the skin with chemicals such as Dihydroxyacetone (DHA) or with natural extracts such as walnut oil. Both ingredients chemically react with the skin's own natural proteins to stain the *stratum corneum* or surface layer.

To achieve the best results, exfoliate skin with a gentle body scrub to slough away dead skin cells and to provide a smooth, even surface. Next wipe skin with toning lotion – a slightly acid pH will ensure a better colour result. Or you can use a moisturiser if you prefer. To avoid streaks, sure that it is fully absorbed before you apply the self-tan. Another foolproof tip is to mix your self-tan with a

little body lotion and then apply it. This way you'll get a lighter, more natural overall colour. If you are using fake tans on your face, avoid your hairline and your eyebrows, particularly if you have blonde or light brown hair. You can mask eyebrows with a little Vaseline to avoid discolouration. Never apply self-tanning products to the soles of your feet and always wash hands thoroughly after applying self-tan as it can stain nails and palms.

And remember. Fake tans only give a small degree of additional sun protection, if any, so always ensure that you still use an appropriate sun protection factor if you intend to sunbathe.

AFTER SUN SOOTHERS

Theoretically, if you use the correct sun protection product, you will protect your skin from burning. However, most of us get caught out from time to time, forgetting to reapply our sunscreen after swimming or just staying out in the sun too long. If you do happen to burn your skin, don't panic. Applying a soothing after-sun or soaking in a cool bath will help to calm sunburn. If your skin is uncomfortable, add a few chamomile herbal tea bags or a handful of chamomile flowers to a pint of warm water, let it infuse, then pour the infusion into a cool bath and relax in it for about 15 minutes. Essential oils of lavender and rose are also excellent sunburn soothers. Drop 3-4 drops of lavender essential oil into a cool bath and soak for 10-15 minutes.

Aloe vera gel, cocoa butter, walnut and avocado oil also help to soothe and remoisturise sun-parched skin. Massage gently into slightly damp skin for best results.

10 SAFE TANNING POINTS

● Protect your skin from inside and take a beta-carotene supplement at least a week before and during your holiday. Beta-carotene is thought to protect the skin from cancer.
● When sunbathing, consider the following points: your location – the sun's rays are most powerful close to the equator; the time of day – fair skins should avoid sun between 11 a.m. and 3 p.m.; and the reflection of the sun's rays – ultraviolet bounces off sand, water, shiny or white surfaces, so you can burn in the shade.
● Limit your time in the sun to 10–15 minutes on the first day, increasing your exposure time by 10–15 minutes each day. Even if you have naturally dark or black skin, you should never sunbathe for more than one hour during the first five days of your holiday.
● Always use a high SPF of at least 10 for the first five days. For total safety, never drop below SPF 6.
● Use a water-resistant product while in the water and remember to reapply your sun product immediately after swimming. Towel dry skin and then smooth on an even layer.
● Always use an after-sun cream or lotion to cool skin and to remoisturise after exposure. Look out for those that contain soothing aloe vera and anti-ageing liposomes.
● Protect ultra-delicate areas, such as the ears, lips, nose, eyelids and nipples, with a total block to avoid painful sunburn.
● Reapply your sun product regularly, ensuring you have covered all areas evenly.

SUN PROTECTION CHART

Skin type and natural protection time (NPT) in minutes	U.K./northern Europe	SPF Mediterranean	The tropics
Children and ultra-sensitive skins – red hair, fair hair, freckled skin NPT= 5 mins	10–8 first days then 8	15–10 first days then 10	Total block then 25–20
Fair skin and skin that burns easily NPT=10 mins	10–8 first days then 6	15–10 first days then 8	20–15 first days then 15
Moderately sensitive, tends to burn, then tans normally NPT=15 mins	8–6 first days then 6	10–8 first days then 8	15–10 first days then 10
Tans easily, burns minimally NPT=20 mins	6 at all times	8 first days then 6	10 first days then 8
Dark skin, rarely burns, e.g. Asian and black skin NPT=30–40 mins	4–6	6	8

CHAPTER NINE

NATURE POWER

Get back to nature and take the plunge with the latest beauty treatments. Thalassotherapy, hydrotherapy and balneotherapy are just a few of nature's cures that use water, seaweed and mud to restore and revive aching limbs, lacklustre skin and a fatigued body. The therapeutic properties of both spring and sea water offer intensive and revitalising benefits for body, mind and soul. Active, body-conscious Europeans now flock to spas to bathe and shower in mineral-rich spring and sea waters. Pour it, splash it, spray it or bathe in it – water has extraordinary powers. It can tone muscles, enliven your complexion, wake you up, calm you down, help cure ills and encourage good health. Why not take to the spa or pamper yourself at home? Turn on the taps, shower or hose pipe and soak up the instant benefits.

AQUA VITAE
THE HEALING PROPERTIES OF WATER

The sea has always possessed mystic healing powers and, despite modern pollution problems, it has retained the ability to cure us of many ailments. Whether it is the plankton- and mineral-rich water itself, or its crop of nutrient-rich seaweeds and plants, the sea has a veritable wealth of health and beauty secrets.

There is no doubt that we have a great affinity with water and many evolutionists believe man's aquatic past is accountable for our love of water. The world-famous obstetrician and water birth expert, Dr Michel Odent, believes that water holds the cure to a myriad of health problems. It soothes us, stimulates us, makes us feel sensual and protected, giving us sensations similar to those that we experienced in the womb. He also believes in the healing properties of water and suggests that the growing trend towards spa visits and water therapy could represent a desire to return to our aquatic past.

The healing power of water is not a modern concept by any means. The Greek dramatist, Euripides, claimed that the sea could provide a cure for man's ills, as did the 18th-century English doctor, Richard Russell. And today, the French, Japanese, Americans, Germans and British are all flocking to the water in the belief that it can treat the stresses and strains of 20th-century life.

THALASSOTHERAPY

If you thought that sea water was just a salty solution, think again. It contains all the elements essential for life – an environment of different composites that ensure a permanent balance, comparable to the constant chemical humoral of our own blood and interstitial plasma. This balance in man is constantly exhausted and has to be restored by the intake of food, water and oxygen. Sea water also has an abundance of essential minerals, plus a wealth of trace elements and organic substances, which extensive medical research has shown to be capable of restoring and preserving good health. The main component of sea water is sodium chloride or salt, combined with sulphur, magnesium, calcium, potassium, bromide, strontium and silicum. Other minerals present include iron, copper, aluminium and zinc, along with nutritive salts such as nitrates, phosphates and silicates. The sea is also rich in biological elements and is a plentiful reservoir of plankton, marine bacteria and seaweeds.

Health spas, especially those offering thalassotherapy treatments, have become the New Age mind and body retreats. Thalassotherapy, from the Greek *thalassa* meaning sea, incorporates a variety of therapeutic treatments all using one essential element – sea water. The first thalassotherapy centre was founded by Dr René Bagot at Roscoff in Brittany. Bagot believed that the minerals and trace elements present in sea water were similar to those in our own blood plasma and that our bodies could absorb the minerals from the water by osmosis, especially when the water was heated to body temperature. His research backed up his theories and now doctors all over the world are employing the treatments that he pioneered.

In France, orthodox medical doctors have been researching the effects of thalassotherapy for over 30 years and have set up a Federation of Sea and Health, a central bank of information and research into the effects of sea water and seaweed on a wide variety of illnesses. Dr Paule Obel, a leading French thalassotherapy expert, uses water successfully to treat everything from fatigue to rheumatism, heart disease to hypertension.

DEEP SEA TREATS

Thalassotherapy centres offer a wide range of treatments, including sea water baths, underwater massage and exercises, seaweed and sea mud body wraps, and pressurised jets of water.

These treatments aim to stimulate the circulation, alleviate fatigue, and eliminate the toxins that can build up and lead to cellulite. At Casablanca's Le Lido Institute of Thalassotherapy, the sea water comes from the African Atlantic, and is particularly rich in minerals and thermal plankton. The course of treatment, or 'cure', runs over six days, with around four treatments per session. Treatments include Le Jet Sous-Marin, which comprises a series of underwater exercises performed while a water jet pummels various parts of the body and helps to detoxify and stimulate the circulation while breaking down accumulated fatty deposits; and La Grande Douche à Jet, which consists of being showered from top to toe in warm sea water with a high-pressure hose. Again, this stimulates the circulation and breaks down cellulite. Other treatments include seaweed body wraps and bubbling jacuzzi baths, which cleanse the system of any toxins.

At The Seawater Treatment Centre at La Baule in the south of Brittany, you can experience similar deep-cleansing sea water and seaweed treatments. The centre specialises in beauty treatments developed by thalassotherapy experts Thalgo, who have created an extensive range of sea beauty products, many of which can also be used at home. The centre offers underwater massage jets, water physiotherapy, underwater massage, turbo baths, a range of seaweed-based skin treatments, and jet massage showers.

At the luxurious Biotherm spa in Deauville, Normandy, sea water and seaweed treatments are used to rejuvenate and revitalise. Experience treatments such as the Bain Bouillonnant, a bubbling bath with multiple pressure jets that massage the body and stimulate the metabolism. Many therapists believe that this type of treatment even encourages mineral uptake. One of Biotherm's specialities is the 'enveloppement d'algues', which comprises being smothered from top to toe in a creamy seaweed paste and wrapped up in layers of plastic, NASA-designed insulating foil and a blanket, and left to relax for up to half an hour until the minerals are absorbed. Biotherm offer a wide selection of 'cures' including the 'cure énergie', which comprises cleansing and revitalising facials, thalassotherapy treatments and massage; and the 'cure minceur', a slimming and body-firming package, which concentrates on ridding you of unwanted cellulite by stimulating your circulation with massage and thalassotherapy. Also on offer are three-day anti-stress and post-natal programmes, again including a selection of treatments that depend on your specific needs. Unfortunately the centre is closed at present for extensive rebuilding works but it is worth remembering for a luxurious treat in future years.

At the Thalassotherapy Institute and Hotel in Quiberon, France, an abundance of rejuvenating hydrotherapy treatments are available. At the Institute, there are literally hundreds of private cabins, with sea water baths, body-pummelling showers and high-pressure jets, and all kinds of soothing and stimulating massage that aims to revitalise, firm, tone and refresh the body and skin. For further information, contact the Thalassotherapy Institute and Hotel, BP 170, 46170, Quiberon, France.

Mineral-rich seawater rejuvenates body and soul and leaves the skin feeling firm and toned.

A SALTY SOLUTION

Mineral-rich waters provide a natural boost for body and soul. The water of Israel's Dead Sea is unique, with a mineral concentration about 10 times greater than any other sea. In the early 50s, Professor Dostrowsky of the Dermatology Department of Israel's Hadassah University advised psoriasis sufferers to bathe in its waters and in the hot springs of Ein Bokek on its shores. The results were encouraging, and now hundreds of sufferers make their pilgrimage to these waters each year. Some European hospitals even sponsor visits. Such success cannot be attributed to the super-saturated salt solution alone. Solar treatment also seems to play an important role. The Dead Sea lies 394 metres below sea level and much of the sun's burning UVB rays are dispersed before they reach the earth's surface. This means that skin can be exposed to sunlight for long periods without fear of burning. Psoriasis clears up completely in some sufferers, while others experience considerable

Thalassotherapy centres offer invigorating sea water treatments involving refreshing jets of water. Therapists are able to control the pressure and temperature depending on the desired effect.

improvements without the use of other medication. You can reap some of the benefits of this mineral-rich oasis by adding salts extracted from the Dead Sea to your bath. In addition to alleviating many skin complaints, the salts relieve aches and pains, relax the muscles, leave skin refreshed, and boost the circulation.

SEAWEED TREATS

Like sea water, seaweed possesses potent healing powers. Seaweed has existed since the beginning of life on earth and its importance in the sea is primordial. As a result of the process of photosynthesis, seaweed produces a wide variety of organic substances, sugars and amino acids, as well as releasing oxygen from carbonic gases that dissolve in water. Scientists believe that seaweed produces 70 per cent of the earth's oxygen.

Sea plants contain concentrated amounts of oligo elements, or trace minerals, found in the ocean, and have a healthy cocktail of vitamins A,

B, C, D, E and K. Seaweed contains chlorophyll, which allows it to use solar energy and enables it to synthesize the organic substances that it needs for nourishment. Although there are over 25,000 types of seaweed, only 10 of them are commercially harvested. An important part of the staple diet of the Japanese, seaweed and sea vegetables are thought to protect against heart disease and recent research also shows that sea plants can protect us from some of the harmful effects of pollution. One of seaweed's main components, alginic acid, has the ability to bind with harmful waste materials in our body and aid their elimination from our system. Seaweed is also rich in iodine, which is essential for proper metabolic functioning. Thyroxine, the hormone that is the master controller of the metabolism, is produced by the thyroid gland from iodine. Iodine is also thought to protect the body against radioactivity, which can contribute to premature ageing. In addition, seaweeds are thought to reinforce the immune system, contain antibiotic elements, stimulate the thyroid gland and encourage the body to burn fat more efficiently. Seaweed supplements, such as kelp, can be useful in guarding the body against pollution. A rich source of protein, seaweed is also low in fat and, although an acquired taste, it is an interesting alternative to land-cultivated vegetables and an excellent accompaniment to seafood. Investigate seaweed recipes, particularly in macrobiotic and Japanese cuisine. Dried seaweeds are available from most health food shops and Oriental food suppliers.

Seaweed possesses a number of healing and therapeutic qualities, which are now being fully exploited by both orthodox and complementary practitioners.

SKIN DEEP

The molecular structure of the elements in seaweed allows them to pass into our body through the skin, in a similar way to that of sea water. Many of the seaweed treatments available are detoxifying, stimulating and deep-cleansing. The oligo elements present in these plants are also compatible with our skin and help to protect, soothe, firm and stimulate, while removing toxins and neutralising free radicals.

Most of the seaweeds used in these preparations are cultivated and harvested along the Brittany coastline in France. To preserve the nutrients,

combat oxidation and bacterial contamination, plants are lypholised or freeze-dried. When water is added to it, the minerals and vitamins are re-activated.

WRAP UP

One of the most luxurious and beneficial seaweed body treatments is the body wrap or mask. A thick paste of seaweed is applied to the body from top to toe, although some therapists avoid using it on the breasts. You are then wrapped in several layers of plastic and blankets to retain the heat, or left in a warm room to encourage the penetration of the oligo elements.

SOAK IT UP

Bathing in seaweed baths can alleviate a multitude of minor ailments, from period pains to muscular tension, as the deep action of the plants' components helps to soothe, cleanse and detoxify. Balneotherapy, or bath treatments, are an essential

SEAWEED
- It is re-mineralising and helps to reinforce our natural immune system.
- It helps to eliminate various toxins from the body, via the skin or the urinary system.
- It can stimulate the metabolism and the endocrine glands.
- According to many researchers, it has both antibiotic and anti-ageing properties.
- It stimulates the blood circulation.
- It stimulates the thyroid gland and encourages the burning up of fat.

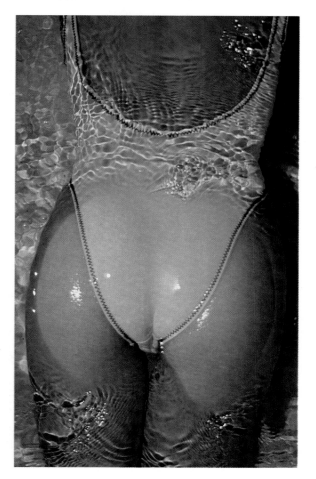

Soak away tension in hot, bubbling water to leave you feeling deeply relaxed.

part of the treatment programme at thalassotherapy centres but you can also reap the benefits at home with a variety of seaweed soaks. Seaweed-based skin preparations help to cleanse, pep up circulation, moisturise and rebalance.

Seaweed not only treats the body and skin, but also revitalises lacklustre tresses. Nourishing the hair itself and cleansing and stimulating the scalp, seaweed shampoos and conditioners are instant hair revivers.

HYDROTHERAPY

Sea water treatments are not the only form of water therapy available. Hydrotherapy, which quite simply involves the use of water, usually from a mineral spring, can be equally beneficial. The man largely responsible for reviving faith in its powers was the 19th-century Bavarian priest Sebastian Kneipp. He recovered from tuberculosis after taking water therapy and went on to develop more than 100 treatment methods.

Today, these are used in spas and hospitals all over Europe to improve skin condition, stimulate sluggish circulation, and protect against illness. Kneipp hydrotherapy uses water from thermal springs or plain fresh water to stimulate the skin and, by way of the nervous system and blood vessels, the internal organs. Temperature is all-important to the technique. The greater the difference in water temperatures used, the greater its effects should be.

DIY HYDROTHERAPY

The Kneipp method bible, the *Vademecum Pro-medico*, lists appropriate temperature levels (cold water 10–12°C, lukewarm 18–20°C, warm 36–38°C and hot 40–42°C), as well as the various treatment techniques, many of which you can do in your own home. Make sure you consult your doctor before taking any strenuous treatments and take note of Kneipp's golden rules.

● Never apply cold water to a chilled body. Warm up first by exercising gently or taking a warm shower. Skin should respond quickly to cold water by tingling and glowing pink, so there's no need to use it for more than about 30 seconds.

● If you have been ill or feel delicate, begin by using warm water, then change to alternating warm (38°C) and cold (10–16°C) applications before progressing to cold alone.

● After treatment, wipe away excess water with your hands. Only towel-dry areas of the body that won't be covered with clothing. Wrap up warmly in natural fibres (cottons and wools) that allow skin to breathe freely.

● After cold treatments, go for a brisk 10-minute walk to generate body warmth. After lukewarm or warm baths, tuck yourself up in bed and rest for at least half an hour.

Kneipp techniques to carry out at home include Affusion and Blitzguss. Affusion consists of a gentle stream of running water being poured over the skin. Best results are achieved with a low-pressure hose held about 10 cm (4 inches) away from the body. To enliven and firm a tired complexion, direct cold running water at the face. First use circling movements, then spray across the face. Afterwards pat dry with the hands. Blitzguss consists of a high-pressure jet being directed at various areas of the body, such as the bottom and thighs, to speed up circulation. Some therapists say this also helps shift cellulite. Most use powerful sprays for the treatment, but an ordinary hand-held shower will do. Take a warm shower first. Switch to cold water for 20 seconds, back to warm for a minute or two, then end with another blast of cold. For building resistance to minor ills and generating vitality, spray the entire body. Start with the face, move down the arms and legs, then the chest and stomach, and finally down the back. Therapeutic herbs are always added to Kneipp baths. Buy them

The tonic effect of hydrotherapy treatments leaves the skin glowing and invigorated. By stimulating the circulation, the body's natural elimination processes are also speeded up, helping to flush away toxins.

fresh, wrap in muslin and hang them from the tap so they steep in the water. Kneipp's favourites included valerian (to soothe), spruce needles (to refresh and restore), chamomile (to soothe inflammation and ease tension), rosemary (to stimulate circulation and revive), and thyme (to help fight infection).

THERAPEUTIC BATHS

No-one can deny the soothing effect of a warm bath. A relaxing and cleansing bath at home can be just as therapeutic as at a spa or thalassotherapy centre. Always take a warm rather than hot bath – the temperature of the water should be around 36–38°C, no higher. This should help you unwind and sleep soundly. A bath that is too hot can actually leave you feeling weak and drained of energy. It can also raise blood pressure and over-dilate blood capillaries. For a stimulating treat, shower with warm water, then run a warm bath. While the bath is filling, massage a couple of handfuls of natural sea salt on to damp skin. Concentrate on the elbows, knees, hands and feet, then massage into the stomach, thighs, buttocks, back and shoulders. Immerse yourself in the warm water and let the sea salt dissolve. Keep massaging your skin gently with a sisal brush or hemp mitt.

In the summer or to refresh you, a cool bath can also work wonders. Use water around 32–35°C and add six to eight drops of uplifting essential oil, such as melissa, neroli or lemon. Shower with warm water afterwards. You could also try a do-it-yourself sitz bath, a type of bath common at European spa resorts. Run enough warm or cool water to enable you to sit in the bath without the water rising above waist level. Wrap your torso in a warm towel, covering your chest, back, shoulders, neck and arms. Sit in the bath for about 10 minutes. Sitz baths help to promote restful sleep, aid relaxation and boost the circulation.

A cold bath is very refreshing and soothing but only try it if you're feeling brave. Sit in the water up to the waist only, to wake up your system and to cool irritated or sunburnt skin. Cold baths are not advisable for those who are suffering from heart conditions.

HEALING WATERS

Spa waters are believed to be especially therapeutic. The Chinese, Japanese, American Indians, ancient Greeks and Romans all knew the benefits of water therapy. Hot and cold springs have been frequented for centuries and are renowned for their healing properties. The word spa originates from the Belgian town of Spa, which was a fashionable mineral spring resort in the 18th century. The Roman town of Aquae Sulis, meaning 'waters of the goddess Sul' and known today as Bath, was one of Britain's most popular spa resorts, where people could not only bathe in the spring water but drink it too. The naturalist Pliny the Elder extolled the curative powers of thermal waters around the Italian town of Bormio back in the first century, and local lore describes their value in treating gynaecological problems, especially infertility. The water that gushes from springs dotted around the town has a naturally high temperature, around 38–43°C. Melting snow and rain water seep through the dolomite rocks, collecting mineral deposits along the way. It falls several thousand feet into the earth, where it is heated up before being spewed up to the surface. The old Roman baths at Bormio's spring have remained unchanged to this day. Here you can soak away aches and pains collected on the piste (the area is a well-known skiing resort) while inhaling the steam, said to help treat respiratory ailments such as rhinitis, laryngitis, bronchitis and asthma. At the nearby Bagni Vecchi, there is a 'sweating grotto', where the flowing thermal waters create a natural underground sauna. It is the only one of its kind in the alpine chain and, compared to traditional Swedish saunas, the temperature is cooler and the air more humid, so making it easier to tolerate for longer periods of time. The gentle perspiration it induces helps eliminate unwanted toxins through the pores. Cold water showers taken at regular intervals leave skin tingling and feeling exceptionally clean and bright. The Terme Bormiesi in Bormio is another popular centre. Built some 20 years ago, it boasts a huge thermal water swimming pool and whirlpool, ozonised hydromassage baths, mud baths, saunas, and steam inhalation units.

Famous for its pure, unadulterated spring water, Evian, situated on the shore of Lake Geneva, is the ideal place to recuperate and be rejuvenated. At the Centre Evian Equilibre, you can experience a wide variety of water cures and hydrotherapy treatments based on the healing properties of water. Evian's water comes from the northern Alps of Haute-Savoie and takes 15 years to pass through a natural filter of various rocks and sediments. Offering a perfect balance of mineral salts and rich in calcium, magnesium and bicarbonates, Evian water is low in both sulphates and sodium and is therefore suitable for the majority of dispositions.

Enjoy a myriad of ultra-modern treatments including jet sprays, underwater massage, carbogaseous baths, and seaweed and fangotherapy (mud) body wraps. Relax in the space-age chamber, which consists of a cabin containing a water bed on which you lie while listening to soothing music and watching hypnotic lights. At the Crenotherapy Institute, the main treatment available is the intensive water-drinking cure, known as 'diuresis'. Lasting three weeks, this cure increases the level of urine, which in turn encourages kidney function; reduces the urine's acidity and its level of calcium and other minerals that might cause kidney stones; helps to improve the elimination of urea, uric acid and other body wastes; and is of particular benefit to anyone suffering from chronic urinary infection. The French Health Authorities actually recognise the success of the cure at Evian and recommend it for many ailments. Evian also offers special packages for people wishing to lose weight, recuperate after illness or shape up after having a baby. The Mother and Baby weeks are particularly successful and include swimming, underwater treatments, beauty treatments, baby massage and development activities, together with exercise and relaxation for both mother and baby. For further information, contact Centre Evian Equilibre, 74500, Evian, France, Tel. 010 33 50 75 02 30.

(For further information about other mineral spas, turn to pages 142–143.)

Cool water showers taken at regular intervals leave the skin tingling, clean and bright.

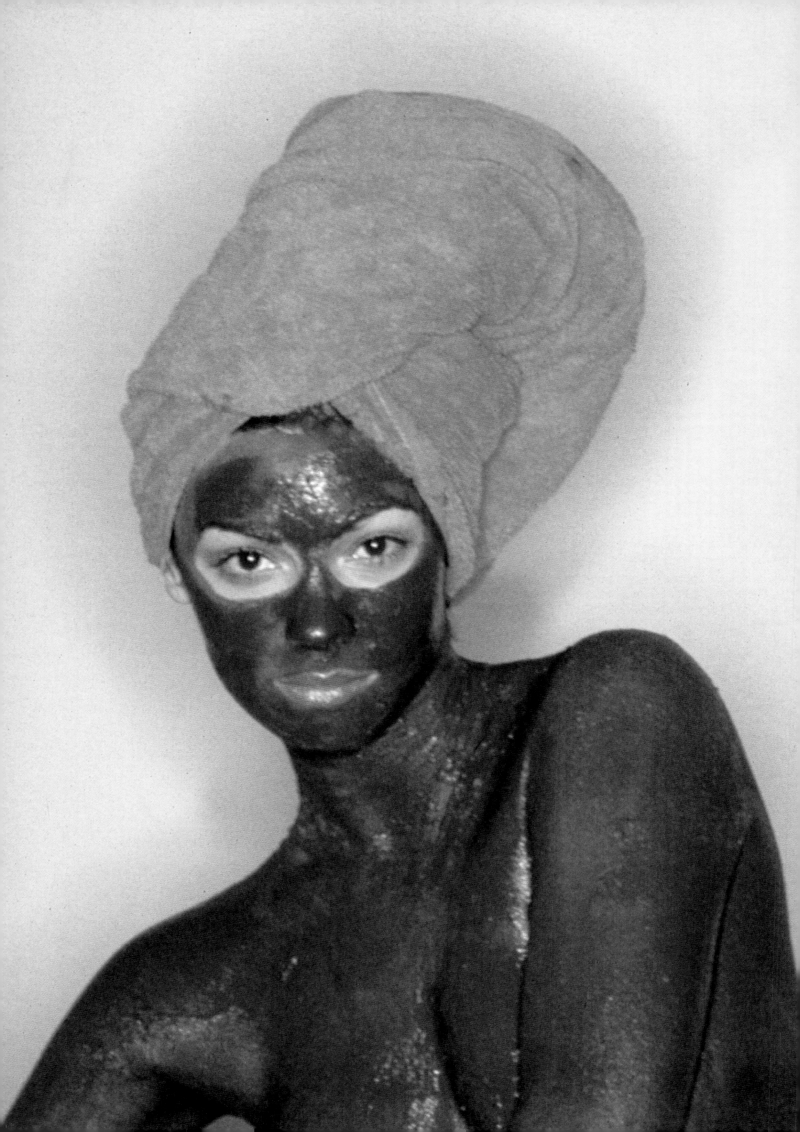

EARTHY POWERS
THE BENEFITS OF MUD

Like seaweed, mud has been used for centuries to cleanse and revive both face and body. Renowned for its healing properties, mud is most often used to alleviate the pain associated with arthritis and rheumatism, to soothe muscular tension, and to treat cellulite and acne. It has many different guises but clay is the purest form. Wallowing in all sorts of mud, from kaolin to Fuller's Earth, can greatly benefit body and soul.

These organic treatments, dug deep from the earth and sometimes the sea bed, contain a multitude of skin-enhancing ingredients, from essential minerals and vitamins to nutritive oligo-elements. Mud may be one of the most ancient beauty treatments but its benefits cannot be denied.

The most beneficial property of mud and clay is their ability to act like a vacuum cleaner on the skin's surface, drawing out and absorbing surface debris, such as dead cells, excess sebum and traces of old make-up. Clay and mud particles also carry negatively charged ions, which allow them to attract and pick up positively charged skin impurities. Many are enriched with therapeutic minerals, such as magnesium carbonate and zinc, which help to tone and disinfect the skin, leaving it really deep-cleansed.

Every skin type can reap the rewards of these skin-polishing elements and benefit from a regular application of a clay- or mud-based mask. Oily or combination skins, in particular, will quickly show signs of improvement, as these earthy preparations have a powerful rebalancing effect. Naturally, the mud used is not the kind that you might find in your garden. Different types of mud are found in different locations around the world and each has properties individual to the area of its origin. From volcanic Parafango mud dredged up from the lakes of Padua in Italy to Fango mud from the Montecatini thermal springs in Tuscany, from the mineral-rich mud from the Dead Sea in Israel to Techirghiol Lake mud near the Black Sea in Russia, this organic substance is rich in many vegetable and mineral extracts, such as bromine, magnesium and potassium.

Mud from the Dead Sea contains salts that are ten times more concentrated than those in ordinary sea water. It also has a unique mineral composition comprising large amounts of potassium, magnesium and bromine. Scientists working at the Institute of Physical Medicine and Balneology (the study of bathing and mineral springs) at Giessen University in Germany, have decreed Dead Sea mud to be highly therapeutic. It not only acts as an effective cleanser and moisturiser, but is also thought to alleviate certain forms of psoriasis and eczema. Smooth on to clean, slightly damp skin and massage in, leaving it to dry. Remove gently with a damp sponge and spray skin with spring water before toning and moisturising.

The most popular forms of mud treatments are mud baths and poultices. Parafango mud is most often used as an all-over body pack or a poultice. It is heated and then cooled, before being applied to the hands, feet, knees, elbows and shoulders. Mud tends to retain heat, so it keeps the water at a constant temperature for as long as 20 minutes.

HOME MUD TREATS

Concoct your own clay and mud treatments by using kaolin and Fuller's Earth. Treat dry skin to a rehydrating face pack by blending 1½ tablespoons of Fuller's Earth (available from chemists and health food shops) with 2 teaspoons of avocado oil, 1 teaspoon of honey and 1 egg yolk. Combine in a blender until smooth and apply to cleansed skin. Leave on for 5–10 minutes and rinse off with warm water. Apply a moisturiser.

Revitalise normal skin by blending 1 tablespoon of Fuller's Earth with 6 drops of essential oil of rose or chamomile and 200 ml (7 fl oz) of spring water. Apply to skin and leave on for 5–10 minutes. Rinse thoroughly with warm water.

Oily skin can also benefit from purifying mud treatments. Combine 1½ tablespoons of Fuller's Earth with 2 drops of essential oil of basil and 2 drops of lemon essential oil, and stir in ½ carton of natural low-fat yoghurt. Leave on skin for 15 minutes and rinse away with warm to cool water. Pat skin dry.

Face and body can benefit greatly from do-it-yourself mud treatments. For the best results, apply mud based face and body packs to warm, dampened skin. This will aid detoxification and help remove any impurities. For those with sensitive skin, adding a few drops of rose or chamomile essential oil can offer a soothing bonus. It is also a wise idea if your skin has sensitive tendencies to keep the mask damp by spraying at intervals with mineral water to prevent it drying out completely.

INDEX

CREDITS

PHOTOGRAPHIC CREDITS

Bensimon, Gilles
pages 2, 7, 37, 76/77, 124;

Browar, Ken
pages 14, 16, 24, 32, 52, 60, 66,
75, 79, 81, 83, 89, 97, 104, 105,
114, 115, 136, 138;

Feurer Hans
pages 80, 91, 98/99, 102/103,
126/127, 128;

Gstalder, Christof
page 133;

Hanson, Pamela
pages 58/59;

Kettiger, Christian
pages 22/23, 122/123;

Kohli, Eddie
pages 106/107;

Lousada, Sandra
page 67; from the *Complete Book of
Massage* by Clare Maxwell-Hudson.
Published by Dorling Kindersley;

Mácabe, Eamon J.
pages 21, 27, 47, 57, 73, 109, 121,
125, 139;

Macpherson, Andrew
pages 78, 112;

Magni, Tiziano
page 101;

Newton, Phillip
page 116;

Nice, Brian
pages 29, 71, 86, 119, 131;

Schneider, Hans Peter
pages 62, 111, 134;

Shining, Stewart
page 140;

Toscani, Olivero
pages 9, 31, 135;

Wheeler, Simon
page 17;

Whittuck, Andrew
pages 18/19.

ILLUSTRATION CREDITS

Hannaford, Tony
pages 34/35, 36, 38/39, 40/41,
42/43, 44/45, 53, 54/55;

Byrne, Andrea
pages 50/51.

**With thanks to the following
models;**
Karen Alexander, Alexandra,
Anate, Aya, Monica Belucci,
Natalie Bloom, Kersti Bowster,
Carmen, Charmaine, Roberta
Chirko, Dionne, Dorothy, Emma,
Emma S, Famke, Carol Gerland,
Jade, Looma, Elle Macpherson,
Marielle Macville, Mystee,
Claudia Schiffer, Rene Simonson,
Sophia, Stephanie, Tasha,
Theresa.